a record of awakening

DAVID SMITH

a record of awakening

Practice and Insight on the Buddhist Path

WINDHORSE PUBLICATIONS

Published by
Windhorse Publications
11 Park Road
Birmingham, B13 8AB
e-mail: windhorse@compuserve.com
web: www.fwbo.org/windhorse

Printed by
Interprint Ltd
Marsa, Malta

Design Dhammarati
Cover photo Jill Furmanovsky

British Library Cataloguing in Publication Data:
A catalogue record for this book is available
from the British Library
ISBN 1 899579 05 2

Contents

Acknowledgements

I would like to express my gratitude to Sara, Vessantara, and all at Windhorse Publications, for helping me put together this work. Their selfless effort is testament to their practice of the Buddha Dharma. Also to the Venerable Sangharakshita for his encouragement and help, and to the Venerable Hitesi for his sympathetic-joy and useful comments and suggestions regarding Part 1.

David Smith

Preface

In the autumn of 1997 I received, out of the blue, a draft copy of a booklet that used as its framework the Ten Stages of Bodhisattvahood. The booklet was accompanied by a letter in which the author, David Smith, requested that I might find time to read it and then let him know what I thought, as he would value my judgement greatly. He went on to inform me that he had been a practising Buddhist for twenty years, and that the 'unfolding of the Dharma', and the experience and insight he had tried to express in the booklet, had taken place during the short while that he was a monk in Sri Lanka, after having done his formative training in the Zen tradition in London, where he now lived.

People often sent me manuscripts to read and comment on, and sometimes these were so bulky that I had to put them to one side for several weeks or even months. My unknown correspondent's 'Practice and Insight on the Bodhisattva Path' consisted of only 14,000 words, and as his letter had, moreover, aroused my curiosity, I read it almost immediately and at a single sitting.

It was a remarkable document. The first thing that struck me about it was the fact that it was a record of the author's own living experience, as he called it. Nowadays hundreds of books on Buddhism are available in all the major Western languages. Most of these are either of a purely academic nature or rehashes of existing works. Only a few of them are based on personal experience, and only too often the experience itself is one-sided and the claims made on its behalf immoderate. David Smith's booklet, on the contrary, was the fruit of more than twenty years of Buddhist practice – a practice that evidently had been both deep and comprehensive; and though the experiences and insights of his time in Sri Lanka were, no doubt, extraordinary, he wrote about them in a style that was sober and down-to-earth.

As I went through the draft of his booklet, that autumn day in 1997, I was irresistibly reminded of the *Platform Scripture*, the reading of which had played such an important part in my own 'awakening' (to use David Smith's language) nearly fifty years ago. Like Hui Neng, David Smith was no scholar. In his own words, he was 'just an ordinary working-class chap with average intelligence and an ordinary education', and one who carried around, moreover, 'as much "baggage" as most Western people do'. Like Hui Neng he was consistent and uncompromising in his commitment to the Dharma, and like Hui Neng he had only a limited acquaintance with the Buddhist scriptures.

The only scripture he actually mentioned in his draft was the *Lankāvatāra Sūtra*, and even this he mentioned only indirectly, when expressing his 'eternal gratitude' to D.T. Suzuki's important and influential *Studies* in that work. His scheme of the ten *bhūmis* or stages of the Bodhisattva Path appeared, however, to be taken from the *Daśabhūmika Sūtra*, though his experience as he progressed through the bhūmis as far as the seventh, on which he was still working, had not tallied with those described in the sūtra. Indeed, at the outset of his booklet he declared bluntly that the little he had come across in the scriptures on the subject of the Bodhisattva Path and the ten stages had been neither useful nor accurate. Ninety percent of it had not conformed to his experience. He did not, I noted, say that his experience had not conformed to what he had found in the scriptures.

Nevertheless, I was struck by the essential orthodoxy of his position, even though some of his expressions might not have been in accordance with the strict letter of Buddhist tradition. I was also struck by his insistence that, after what he called awakening, the everyday, deluded mind continued to exist, alongside the Awakened Mind, and that from the first bhūmi to the last there was a great struggle, or 'holy war', between these two minds, as the former sought to transform, and free itself from, the latter. Obviously this corresponded to the well-known division between the Path of Vision and the Path of Transformation, though David Smith's description of the relation between the two was more dramatic than mine, and though he envisaged awakening not in terms of Stream Entry but, apparently, in terms of the Arising of the (real) Bodhicitta. At the same time, 'awakening was neither "Zen" nor "Theravada", but a merging of the two – with an extra flavour.' In his own living experience he had, it seemed, succeeded not just in synthesizing, but even in transcending, the two separate traditions, at least in respect of their separateness. He was also concerned to emphasize that a strong concentration was essential as a prerequisite to insight, that insight could be developed in connection with dreams, that bowing was an important spiritual practice, and that one should not believe that only monks could attain insight. One could practise the Dharma perfectly well in lay life.

By the time I finished reading 'Practice and Insight on the Bodhisattva Path' I felt that I had come across a treasure. I felt that through the booklet I was in contact with a fellow Dharma-farer, even a kindred spirit, and was anxious to meet him in the flesh. At the end of his letter he had said that he looked forward to my reply and that if I should think a meeting would be necessary he would be grateful for that also. As it happened, I had already made arrangements to spend some time in London the following month, and wrote to my unknown correspondent accordingly. The result was that one afternoon he came to see me at my flat in the London Buddhist Centre.

In his booklet David Smith had described himself as being 'just an ordinary working-class chap', and indeed that was what the robust, cheerful, fiftyish man sitting opposite me in my study looked like. Passing him on the street, one probably would not have given him a second glance. All the more remarkable, therefore, was the contrast between the ordinariness of his outward appearance and the extraordinariness, as I knew it to be, of his inner experience. It transpired that he lived alone in his flat in East London, that he worked as a gardener, and that he continued with his practice with the same inner determination as ever. In my letter I had told him that publication of the booklet could certainly be considered, but that the text would need more than the 'bit of a polish' he had in mind. Not that I was suggesting any actual rewriting, I had added, so much as a placing of the text within an explanatory framework. This framework, as I now proceeded to make clear, should include particulars of his life and background and an account of how he first came in contact with the Dharma. This suggestion met with David's ready acceptance. He also accepted my offer to submit 'Practice and Insight on the Bodhisattva Path' to Windhorse Publications (it was unlikely that a non-specialist publisher would be interested), together with a strong recommendation that they publish it. The decision whether or not to publish, I was careful to emphasize, rested entirely with them. I could only recommend.

Months passed. Like the mills of God, the wheels of a publishing house turn slowly, and it was not until early this year that Windhorse eventually decided to publish David's booklet. They also decided that the little work did, indeed, need a framework, and Dharmachari Vessantara, a senior member of the Western Buddhist Order and author of *Meeting the Buddhas*, was commissioned to interview David and in this way elicit the required information. In the event, the interviewer did not confine himself to asking for particulars of David's life and background, so that the edited transcript of the interview amounts to 16,000 words, 2,000 more than 'Practice and Insight on the Bodhisattva Path' itself. It forms Part II of *A Record of Awakening*, with the booklet that landed on my desk out of the blue nearly two years ago forming Part I.

When he came to see me recently, on his visiting Birmingham to meet the Windhorse people, David was concerned to emphasize that the two parts were quite separate and distinct, and should on no account be confused. Part I was text, so to speak, and contained all he really wanted to say, while Part II, consisting of his responses to Vessantara's questions, was commentary. Some of those responses were more of the nature of reflections, rather than being based, as was the written part of the book, entirely on his own direct experience.

Reflections or not, David's responses to Vessantara's questions were of considerable interest and value. Having observed people wandering around changing teachers and traditions, and avoiding practice when they were not getting what they thought they should be getting from their efforts, he is emphatic that one should simply 'stay with it'. Willingness to stay with it he considers the most difficult aspect of practice we have to face, because

it means going against the current that has carried us
along all our lives. At the same time he is aware of the
need for balance. Dharma practice is practice of the
Middle Way, which means striking a balance between the
extremes of a practice that is rigid and oppressive and one
that is slack and uncommitted. Such a balance is difficult
to strike, but unless it is struck, he believes, real progress
along the Path is not possible.

Practice should also be full time. 'True practice is practice that takes place throughout the day, and indeed
during sleep if possible.' Meditation and life in general
should not be seen as two, the whole purpose of developing Dharmic skills being to cultivate and retain a one-
pointed mind in all activities. As for Westerners being a
special case, and needing to incorporate elements of
therapy and psychology into their practice of the
Dharma, he remains unconvinced. The Dharma is alive
and ever present, and can flow into any situation. It is
whole and complete, with no deficiency that needs to be
made good by some Western psychologist.

David is, in fact, a self-declared traditionalist, who
believes that the practices taught by the different Buddhist traditions put one firmly on the Buddha's path and do
not need any embellishment from outside. He is aware,
however, that the Dharma is not only fluid, but timeless
and transparent. Being transparent, it has no fixed form,
so that the fact that it came from India, and went to
China, does not mean that we have to imitate the Indians
or the Chinese. The Dharma 'transports effortlessly

throughout the world,' he tells Vessantara, 'and takes on the clothes of new cultures in any century.'

Though at present he lives alone, David fully recognizes the importance of spiritual companionship. Besides having our teacher as guide, we should also have around us like-minded people who will support and encourage us in our spiritual practice. Living as we do in the midst of forces that are relentlessly pulling us in the opposite direction, and wanting us to lose ourselves in the world of sensory pleasure, it is easy for us to feel isolated as we practise the disciplines we have undertaken. Sangha is also useful in that spiritual friends will challenge any tendency on our part to complacency, taking apart our cherished notions of what constitutes right practice and leaving us, very often, rather deflated.

In what he writes about the Bodhisattva Path, as well as in his responses to Vessantara's questions, David certainly challenges our complacency. In this respect he is a true spiritual friend to the reader. Not that he sees himself as ever being a teacher, as he made clear to me in his original letter. He looks upon his writing – and, no doubt, his answers to questions – 'as being my offering to those who may find it useful in their training and also as testament that it is possible for lay Western people in these times to attain what the heart truly desires.' It was for this reason, he concluded, that he would like to see 'Practice and Insight on the Bodhisattva Path' through to publication.

With the publication of *A Record of Awakening* that wish has now been fulfilled, and it only remains for the rest of us not only to benefit from David's experience and insight, but also to be inspired by the rare example of a life so consistently and so uncompromisingly dedicated to the practice of the Dharma.

Urgyen Sangharakshita
Madhyamaloka
Birmingham
8 June 1999

For my teacher in Sri Lanka,
for offering to take me on as his pupil
so as to encourage me to practise
and ripen the fruit that he knew
was ready to fall.

I

Practice and Insight on the Bodhisattva Path

Introduction to the Bodhisattva Path

In the following pages I will attempt to convey to you my own living experiences of the wonderful journey the Awakened Heart undertakes on the Bodhisattva Path that leads to Buddhahood.

It could never be said that I have scholastic desires, and I have therefore never spent much energy in finding works from the scriptures about this subject of the Bodhisattva Path. In fact precious little has been written or translated on what is doctrinally known as the 'Ten Stages of Bodhisattvahood', so what little I have come across has been neither useful for practice nor accurate. Not useful, in the sense that no knowledge could be gleaned that could help clarify and confirm the insight that has arisen within me; and not accurate, in the sense that ninety percent of it does not conform to my experience.

Much of this could be simply because of the way it is written. I do not pretend to have any understanding of how a Chinese or Indian mind 2,000 years or so ago may have worked. If I did I might be able to see why they articulated their insight mostly from the 'cosmic'

Bodhisattva point of view, and largely ignored their insight from the 'down-to-earth' Bodhisattva point of view! Perhaps they thought it was the best way to pass on their knowledge, or perhaps they couched it in these esoteric terms to put the whole thing out of reach, to surround themselves or their tradition with mystique. In any event, the *Daśabhūmika* ('path of ten stages') *Sūtra* as presented to us now exists only for scholars to argue over; it is pretty useless to practitioners.

Some may say that the practice and insight laid out in the *Daśabhūmika* is too high a Dharma for the ordinary person. Why bother to give it to them in the first place? But this is not so. Dharma practice is Dharma practice, irrespective of the insight attained. The essence and basic 'rules' are exactly the same.

Orthodox Mahāyāna has divided this journey into ten stages, though according to some writings it has been mapped out in fewer. But the actual unfolding of Buddhahood is not experienced in bits or slices. It is a smooth journey that goes ever deeper into the seemingly endless, magnificent delusion that we call saṁsāra.

There are periods when the Awakened Mind looks into a particular aspect of saṁsāra; then, when insight into it is fully matured, it will move into a fresh field. This can be seen as moving on to the next stage. However, sometimes this new stage is not so obviously different from the previous one. A further complication is that there can sometimes be quite a shift within an actual stage. When I was moving through such an experience myself, this would make me think that a new stage had begun. The 'edge' is not so clear.

All in all, these stages seem to me to be mainly for convenience. The Mahāyāna has an obsession with the number ten, and that is why this wonderful natural process has been laid out in this way. It would not take much imagination on my part to come up with dozens of stages, or to condense them into far fewer.

In these notes I wish not only to share some of this wonderful insight, but also to offer it in such a way that it can be of use in daily practice for those who are committed to the Dharma. First I will try to give the structural framework by which the stages are approached by the Awakened Heart, for it is important to have a basic grasp of this.

At the moment of 'coming back to life' after awakening, the Awakened Mind is born. This is sometimes called the Transcendental Mind, among other titles. I shall call it the Mind with a capital M as opposed to the small m of the ordinary everyday deluded mind. Before the awakening there is only the ordinary mind, a mind that by definition is always deluded. After years of practice this mind develops wisdom into the nature of itself and becomes more and more refined in that respect until it finally reaches the point where it cannot know any more about itself, and falls into Equanimity. Shortly after this, awakening takes place, and with that the Bodhisattva Path is alighted upon.

At this stage there is a very important point that I should make. There is a popular misconception that with awakening the everyday ignorant mind is swept away, leaving just the pure wisdom of enlightenment. This notion is profoundly wrong. What remains is a paradox that many will find hard to accept.

The Transcendental is awakened – with all the wisdom of the Buddha complete at the first stage. But shortly after awakening the ordinary small mind comes back to life again, with all its ignorance and power. Well, there is a difference in that it is no longer possible for the awakened person to commit certain acts. But for everyday living one doesn't change much at all.

So here we have the ultimate spiritual paradox: the Mind that knows the truth of existence – the Mind that is awake and soon to be eternally free – living alongside the mind that is ignorance and delusion itself, which will always lead us into suffering in a cycle that has no end. How can we accept such a seemingly impossible truth?

The practice that takes place after the 'breakthrough' is precisely about these 'two' minds. There is an ignorant mind that through its conditioning wants to carry on in exactly the same way it has always done, not concerned about the obvious truth that will often shine through it, and indeed trying to make that wisdom 'mine' at the same time and in all situations. And there is the Awakened Mind that wants to transform and free itself from that very same worldly mind. From the first bhūmi until the last, the Great Struggle of the 'Holy War' is enacted by these two 'players'. This play of two apparent minds may sound completely different from the practice of ordinary practitioners, but in essence it is really the same.

With normal practice we take on a teacher to guide us. If you are really serious about getting to the bottom of suffering don't delude yourself into thinking that it can be done alone. We are always by definition going into the unknown with practice; we cannot know what to expect or do when the depths of our self rise up. We are dealing with powerful forces, and unless we are guided by someone who has walked that way before us, we will flounder. Do not think books will get you out of trouble, either.

But once you are on the Bodhisattva Path, you see the Path at all times and are therefore your own guide – so you are no longer in need of a teacher. Your Transcendental Mind will always see the Way. But that will not impress the deluded mind, which will always carry on as normal because it is nothing but a bundle of karmic sankhāras that acts and reacts in the same old habitual ways.

What follows in these pages will be factual experiences and reflections from just before awakening and then from the first bhūmi to the seventh; this is as far as the 'Advancing Host' has matured to date. All that you read will be nothing but my own living experience.

Insight Meditation

My practice from the beginning was Zen. At the time I was living a lay lifestyle, so the collecting of the heart through daily practice and the development of concentration was always nurtured from within the rough and tumble that this style of living offered. After my move to Sri Lanka in 1980 all this changed.

It is necessary always to try to keep the Eightfold Path in balance. Many Buddhists think that meditation is the be-all and end-all. If you wish only for a peaceful mind, that may be good enough, but to get to the bottom of suffering and change the whole Path has to be embraced. Understanding the practice in daily life is essential. To learn to contain, embrace, and die willingly to the powerful forces of the emotions as experienced in our daily comings and goings is the essential foundation of change. Without this, cultivation of the Path is incomplete and out of balance, and real change cannot take place.

The form of my everyday practice changed radically with the move from lay life to sangha life – not to mention the cultural changes. But – despite the outward change of appearances – in essence the everyday practice never changed at all.

Now that I was in Theravāda robes I remained true to the tradition and dropped the kōan training that had been with me since the beginning of my Zen training. Instead I took up the orthodox Theravāda practice of the Ti-lakkhaṇa, which involves developing insight into anicca, dukkha, and anattā. This had a very profound effect on my meditation.

It was a very free interpretation of this practice with only one real rule: that strong concentration was essential as a prerequisite to insight meditation. Without true samādhi – that is, the dissolution of the dualistic mind – real insight is unlikely to arise, as the self (which can only abide within duality) will always be lurking somewhere to distort, pollute, and possess whatever may arise. With samādhi established, a totally free investigation is allowed to take place.

I have always been blessed with a strong insight faculty, and now with this open approach it was allowed to roam freely through the mind and body, applying any one of the Three Signs of Being to whatever aspect it chose to focus on. It was a disciplined freedom, and it was mar-vellous! – burrowing first this way then that way into the five skandhas with these three 'tools' – my whole mind and body totally dissected, deeper and deeper, insight streaming forth with almost overpowering force. Joy and bliss, and a few tears as well, flowing almost unendingly. Anattā was always my favourite – seeing into all the bits of the mind especially, and seeing that in fact there isn't anyone here at all. Observing the never-ending flow of this mind that is anicca, and seeing the body as part of mind also. Seeing that this mind is in fact everything. And how marvellous dukkha was to observe! In many ways it was the most interesting because of the vast spectrum it covers: on one side the suffering that is inherent in everything, but, on a much deeper metaphysical level, the observation that all things are in constant vibration, which compels constant change (*anicca*).

There was one insight into dukkha that is worthy of mention here. One day I was sitting in deep samādhi. Suddenly awareness dropped like a stone, and came to rest in the very centre of the heart, next to a huge ball of fire. This ball was like the sun. It was round and white with heat, and it hummed like an electricity station. It had immense power. On closer examination it was seen to be fidgeting – a fidgeting caused by intense frustration, as the ball was actually living. It was as if it were being bound and held by something, and not allowed to flow as it desired. Insight showed that this was a part of the life-force and that it was captured and held by ignorant forces within the heart. It wanted so much to follow its nature and flow smoothly, but could only escape when its 'master' allowed it to go, while being caught up with deluded emotional impulses. The life-force is blinded into thinking it is a self and therefore suffers the fears, emotions, and so on, that characterize the self.

This wondrous meditation continued for several months. The mind was like a bird going freely wherever it wished, seeing the lakkhaṇas in everything. It was all joy, happiness, and light. Even wonderful music (the sign of a happy heart) came to my mind and stayed for so long. Throughout that time, the whole notion of the self being a solid undeniable entity that lived in and owned this mind and body was continually being undermined.

Dreams

A large part of my overall experience during those months, and for many months to come, were my dreams. They were to play a large part in the development of insight.

These dreams fell neatly into two halves. Half of them were very joyful – full of indescribable physical bliss. Awareness and alertness were so sharp and alive that they hardly seemed like 'dreams' at all. There was music so loud that the normal ear would have burst, but how wonderful it was! Light and colours so brilliant. Flying through the air – always the great symbol of liberation. There was the letting go of fear in order to achieve the leap into the air, and an acute awareness of what was happening. The searing bliss of this is hard to describe. Sometimes there were walks through beautiful gardens and mansions where the colours and odours were almost overpowering in their splendour. But the greatest characteristic of all was happiness and joy. Yes indeed, the heart was truly happy!

The other half of the dream cycle was the complete opposite. A pattern emerged that ran throughout the whole of this dream episode. A night of no dreams would be followed the next by the blissful dreams I have described. Then on the third night there would be dreams of intense fear and darkness that were profoundly terrifying. On these nights, huge humanoid figures would visit me with just one mission in mind: to kill me. Their mere presence was terrifying enough. They would always start at a distance and then move slowly forwards until one would tower over me and slowly put its hands around my neck and squeeze. Of course the natural impulse would be to pull away, but my body would be paralysed with fear, so fighting was always difficult. Awareness, as in the other dreams, was very sharp. But knowing that 'this is only a dream' didn't help very much.

As the weeks went by I learned to open up to this fear and accept these creatures as my friends. When they came, I would allow them to approach me and take hold of me. I would lie there and say to them 'Okay, if you want to kill me, go ahead.' But the insight was maturing to such an extent that if there was genuine open surrender to the experience of fear, the fear would in time show its true nature. I saw that the pictures around fear – not only in dreams – and the reasons to be afraid, didn't really exist: they were nothing but my own mind's creation. In this case the creatures, the fear, and the dream would fade away and I would fall into deep peaceful sleep. These dreams persisted for a long time, until eventually all fear had gone and the dream itself had been consumed in openness, acceptance, and understanding.

One dream I remember illustrates this new-found wisdom. I was a back-seat passenger in a car travelling at high speed through the streets of my home town, Oxford. As I was familiar with the roads, I knew that if we carried on at this speed we would inevitably crash at the junction just ahead. As fear was building up at my impending death, I was fully aware that I was dreaming – and could abort the dream if I wished. But I decided to go through with the dream, accepting the impending suffering and death. I relaxed into my seat and waited. We came to the junction and crossed over it at high speed, as I thought we would, and ploughed through the window of the shop across the road. My acceptance was complete. I was to die. Then at the last moment the dream broke, and I was catapulted into great bliss and feelings of liberation. The clear knowledge came once again that fear is nothing but a product of the deluded mind, pure and simple. It will fade into nothing if you have the courage to face it with a non-avoiding, accepting, open, embracing mind.

Throughout all this, not once did I see my dreams as being essentially different from my waking state. I saw them as being exactly the same. So the lessons learned from these experiences were easily passed into my daily life. How helpful they were to be in the future!

My first year in Sri Lanka was complete. My practice was very solid, with insight flowing freely from my sitting practice. I felt very happy and balanced. Soon it would be time for the Rains Retreat, so I decided to make good use of the situation and sit a three-month silent retreat alone in my kuṭī.

Everything was organized satisfactorily, and, on the full moon of July, I began. Right at the start, I did something I had never done before. I prostrated myself before my Buddha rūpa and asked for help and guidance as usual, but then spontaneously I made the vow that by the end of the retreat I would be enlightened. How strange that I did such a thing! I have always felt that vow-making can cause trouble and create burdens, especially if the vows are not fulfilled. Determination to do my best had always been good enough in the past. But there you are, it was done, and, strangely enough, I felt good about it.

I settled quickly into the routine and was soon enjoying the wonderful experience of a silent retreat. Two weeks passed and all was going well. Then what I could only describe at the time as a kind of lethargy set in. Try as I might it was impossible to concentrate. Worse, it was getting more and more difficult to muster the energy and will to try. Any effort to 'do' anything was quite impossible. Thoughts simply rose and passed away. There was no interest or attachment or will to go beyond them. A part of me was terribly frustrated, and the thought of spending the next eleven weeks like this made it infinitely worse.

I was not aware of it at the time but in fact the mind had entered 'Saṅkhārā Upekkhā' – Equanimity about Formations. At the time I had no knowledge of this, as I had not studied concepts like that very much. I shall always be very grateful for my ignorance in this area, as I'm sure it would have created problems of attachment at the time if I had known then that this state of mind was the mind needed just prior to awakening. I am sure I would have got unavoidably attached – and therefore lost the path because of anticipation.

Equanimity About Formations

This is the condition of mind that allows awakening to take place. There is much that could be said about it; it is the fruit and pinnacle of practice. This equanimity is the ultimate refinement of the unenlightened mind. It is the 'Middle Way'. It is what true practice of Dharma leads to. It is the fruit of years, indeed lives, of practice.

Now, for a lengthy period of time at least, the mind has learned to let go of what arises within itself, and attains peace. For life after life it has chased these thoughts, driven on by the emotions of the deluded life-force. Now at last it has perfected letting go.

This state has come about through learning and training Dharmic skills, a practice that has gone on for so long. Gradually one learns to contain and not to be carried away by thoughts, feelings, and emotions, over and over again containing these things, until the errant life-force of the heart transforms into understanding and gentleness. The wisdom that arises and deepens through this transforming process comes into life time and again to help contain and transform, all the time deepening.

Slowly, slowly, the mind understands the true nature of itself, and is no longer deceived and driven by the idea of self which is the root and cause of all suffering. With this perfected it falls into Profound Equanimity, at last giving up chasing everything that arises. It even gives up the deep and wonderful wisdom that has grown and deepened – yes, even that, the most precious of possessions.

All that has been learned has to go. Nothing, absolutely nothing, must remain – until you become just like a baby again: innocent, without knowledge, without desires, without aversions, without even non-understanding. When this matures and becomes perfected there is only one natural and inevitable outcome: awakening.

Awakening

For two weeks this state remained, as the equanimity matured more and more. Then on one hot day in August, in the early afternoon, there was a sudden heightened awareness about a few thoughts during meditation – thoughts of nothing in particular – and suddenly consciousness in its entirety vanished, 'winked out'.

Awakening is a short experience that breaks the 'tap root' of ignorance. A tap root is a root found on some plants which, when it is broken, are irreparably damaged. The plant then goes into irreversible decline – though it can look okay for a while. In the same way ignorance too can appear to recover. But even if it takes a few more lifetimes, it will, like the plant, inevitably cease.

It was my understanding from the Pāli scriptures that this 'breaking' is a momentary happening: indeed, that it happens so fast that some people hardly know it has happened, until wisdom arises, when presumably it is known. This momentary happening is possible because, it is said, consciousness arises and passes away moment by moment – and at the end of one of those moments the next one fails to arise, thus giving the 'blip' before the next one does then arise. But for me it was not like this.

It was not a momentary cessation, but lasted much longer – about half a second, I would say. And during the winking out of consciousness there was not a blankness, but a 'knowing'.

Then consciousness came back – not winking back as it had left, but with a kind of rush. After recovering for a minute or so, the Buddha Knowledge started to arise, and continued for several days. Although it flowed smoothly, it came in three main stages, and in the following order.

1. Seeing that there is no person in this mind and body – thus revealing Emptiness.

2. Seeing that from heaven above to hell below, and all in between, all is nothing but a creation of the mind. Furthermore, with the world removed, the forms that remain are not 'solid' objects, but in truth are empty of themselves – thus revealing Profound Emptiness.

3. Seeing that with the removal of self and other, and because of Profound Emptiness, all that Truly 'Is' interpenetrates.

The First Bhūmi

It is hard for me to put into words the feelings of the following minutes. One of the first thoughts seems almost egotistical because of the great feeling of 'victory'. All these years of struggle were not in vain; the training had been true. With this seeing of true training comes the seeing of the Path, a seeing that will never be lost, and will always be there to guide me. And with this came tremendous feelings of gratitude to my teacher for putting me, and keeping me, on the Path of Freedom.

This was the first stage of Bodhisattvahood, and for several days that followed insight rained down almost continuously. So much happened in this time – not just the insight but the feelings of joy and release and many tears of happiness – that it is difficult to remember much of it and the order it all came in.

Certainly one of the first insights was the seeing of the Four Noble Truths with great clarity. Then there was seeing the truth of the great paradox of Mahāyāna – that nothing even exists, and that there isn't even a saṁsāra to be released from. All these years of training were a complete waste of time. So funny, such laughter! What was being seen here was one of the main marks of awakening – Emptiness. Not just emptiness of self, but Profound Emptiness, where form is not just devoid of names and labels, but empty of itself. When this is seen – and the ordinary mind cannot ever see this – all life flows through itself. This is not the 'Oneness' we often hear about but something much more profound even than that.

The very last seeing is the Ultimate seeing, that of Interpenetration. Unlike all the other insights this could never be brought down into the world of thought. It was a seeing, pure and simple. In this the whole universe could be seen contained in any one object. How wondrous, how marvellous! Seeing the Buddhist Society in London nestling comfortably and completely under my fingernail! And that very Buddhist Society within its four walls containing everything that exists – past, present, and even the future, *now*!

My retreat still had ten weeks to go, but I was determined to see it through without changing the routine, slackening in any way, or telling the whole world the 'good news'.

The Mind was so active with reviewing insight and digesting it all. There was overwhelming joy ever present, and great energy flowed to the extent that it was quite impossible to concentrate during meditation. This state of being was to continue for the remainder of the retreat. No matter how much effort was brought forth to tame the mind, it just buckled under the power.

One thing that did become obvious during this time was the tendency to attachment driven by this power. It took every bit of strength and determination to prevent this, I just had to contain it and hold on as best I could. Boy, was 'I' becoming enlightened!

The nature of this process is that after the unfolding of insight the saṁsāric world of ignorance and delusion, like clouds rolling across the clear bright sun, begins to manifest itself again.

Although there could be no doubt about the authenticity of awakening, I was well aware that māra would try to exploit the situation sooner or later, so I decided to undercut the fellow and go to Colombo when the retreat had finished to get confirmation from my Inspirational teacher, who I realized with hindsight knew exactly what was pending several months earlier. After I greeted him and paid my respects, he simply looked at me and smiled.

I then journeyed to a forest araṇya outside Colombo to see an old monk whom I had never met but who had the reputation of great maturity of insight, and who had gathered around him many fine monks with serious and committed practice. I had a long formal interview with him and at the end I asked for confirmation – and he gave it.

After the return to my Bodhi Mandala in the Island Hermitage I felt very much at a crossroads. I felt there was legitimate reason now to give up the practice, as with the 'tap root' broken there can only be a few lifetimes left. I knew that many had taken that decision before me; after all, no matter what might happen in this life, in the overall journey there was now only one direction in which I was going. But for me, it turned out, there wasn't much to consider. The 'job' wasn't finished, and was in fact far from over. I could see that great effort was going to be needed yet again, so I decided to return to the forest dwelling place that I had just left, and to train there alongside, and get support from, the many monks who lived there.

The Tale of the
Wandering Old Man

There was once an old man, a nice, kind, compassionate fellow whose contentment with life would be hard to imagine. He would sit in his rocking chair day after day with a smile on his face, staring into the wood fire, with nothing much to do.

Despite this contentment, somewhere deep inside him there was just a little bit of boredom that would sometimes stir itself ever so slightly. So one day he decided to go for a walk and have a look around, and maybe have a little adventure – something he could never remember having had before.

He dressed himself and off he went. How wonderful it was to be outside in the big world! He walked and walked, totally fascinated by all the wonderful things he saw. Such marvellous scenery with all the hills and trees and rivers, the birds and animals, and so much more. And then there were all the people he met. So many of all shapes and sizes, some kind and some not so kind, and some quite attractive ones too.... On and on he went, being drawn into the wonders of the world, with its colours and shapes and sounds and smells, all so seductive he found it really hard to resist them.

But after some time he began to tire of it all and decided that it was time to go home. So he turned and started back. After a while, though, he realized he couldn't remember his way – he was lost. 'What should I do?' he thought to himself, for he was getting really worried, and he had had enough. At first he enjoyed his experiences but then they seemed to lose their appeal because they weren't quite what they seemed to be. He felt somewhat let down by it all, and decided that being at home was really the best place to be. But what could he do now? He asked many people the way home, and although they tried their best to help, the old man felt that somehow they just didn't know the way – and were, in their own way, just as lost as he was.

He went this way and that, getting more worried and more lost. Then, just as he was at his wit's end, he spotted his home, quite some distance away. On he went, and despite the temptations to get distracted along the way he ploughed on with great will and determination until he dragged himself to his front door. His exciting journey had turned into a nightmare, but now he was home; but as he opened the front door he suddenly woke up! He suddenly realized that from the very beginning he had never even left his home. He had simply fallen asleep and all these seductive experiences had just been his own imagination – just one big dream! Oh, how the old man laughed! As he then once again settled back into his rocking chair, he smiled again in total contentment, and stared into the log fire.

* * *

This story came to me in deep meditation. It could be seen as just an everyday story, or it could be seen as my own journey along the Way – but it didn't come to show me either of those things.

It came to show me that the old man was in fact the Eternal All-Embracing Buddha, and that life is just the eternal dance that he creates for his own enjoyment. He creates life in myriad forms, and loses himself in them, but he makes such a good job of it that he forgets he is only at play. So round and round goes the game and all his creations are forever lost within it. But there is one exception, and that is man. He loses himself in man too, but he also bestows on man the unique ability to reflect. Man enjoys the wonder and mystery of life but, paradoxically, experiences the suffering of it at the same time, and asks himself 'Why?' As that reflective seed develops in some people they soon realize that this life is not what it appears to be, and that is the reason they suffer. Soon they see in truth that life is nothing but a dream, just a play of the mind (*māyā*). And with that settled, each returns Home – to Himself.

Reflections on the Breakthrough

One thing that puzzled me was the apparent comprehensiveness of the knowledge. I had practised Zen for years and easily recognized what is written about awakening in that tradition. While in Sri Lanka I studied to some extent the knowledge as defined in the Pāli Canon, and this I recognized also. In general terms the Pāli Canon focuses on the notion of self and the destruction of the notion that there is a person in this body that says: 'This is me, and this is mine.' With that destruction we are left with just objective dharmas, and a remaining duality. Zen doesn't work with many concepts. It does not focus on the self but scoops it up along with the objective world and destroys the lot, 'leaving' the profundity of Great Emptiness which is the quintessence of Mahāyāna wisdom. And yet with me it all unfolded in a way with which I was completely unfamiliar. I could not understand how this awakening was neither 'Zen' nor 'Theravāda', but a merging of the two – with an extra flavour.

I was on a silent retreat and had no contact with anyone for three months. Also I had denied myself any access to books, so no help from any quarter was forthcoming. I reflected upon the practice. For nearly six years it was the all-embracing spirit of Zen, with a kōan training that kept me focused on that spirit. This was greatly enhanced when, during my first resident sesshin, the first of Zen Master Hakuin's 'Great Deaths' was experienced. The essence of Zen training is the collecting of the life-force which transforms and gentles through practice, and during a sesshin this collecting can be very great and have much power.

One day, under a great surge from this collected life-force, self and other collapsed, revealing Oneness.

It was a profound experience that was characterized by a peace that had no limitations, and that I could only describe as awesome. Although this experience had no wisdom seeing the nature of things, it had a profound effect on me in that it set me straight and true on the Path by removing doubt, and gave me inspiration that would never allow me to give up.

When I took on Theravāda robes the insight work was focused solely on the five skandhas and their dissection within meditation. In hindsight it seemed that this insight needed to mature much more, and this form of practice allowed that to happen. Indeed, because I no longer held on to a concept (kōan), but rather let the concentrated mind roam at will, insight came at such a pace that at times it was almost overpowering. During this time there was little control from me. The concentrated mind seemed to know what it wanted, and it just took over – and did it enjoy itself!

After some months, this practice was complete. Insight into 'self' was complete, and insight that embraced the 'outside' was complete through previous Zen practice. With that done, Sankhārā Upekkhā was entered.

It was as if my practice had been done in two halves, and at awakening the two had merged. It didn't reveal itself in totality, as I suspect it does to the Zen practitioner, and it didn't reveal itself with just the first stratum of awakening as it would with the Theravādin, because there was much more. So what was revealed was outside my previous knowledge of this process – hence the great puzzlement. It is only now that I know it can be categorized as insight according to orthodox Mahāyāna.

It was this comprehensiveness of insight, and the ability to signpost all layers with such clarity, that puzzled me. Then, one day, while pondering this puzzle in deep samādhi, the answer came in the form of an analogy.

The Analogy of the Car Journey

Two people are travelling in a car along a country road. One is driving, the other is a passenger. Together they pass trees, fields, animals, all manner of things, as the car winds its way along the picturesque route.

When they arrive at their destination a friend asks them to describe in detail all they have seen on their journey. First the driver speaks, and he gives a good description of the route: its fields, hills, animals, and so on. His friend is most impressed with his alertness. Then the passenger speaks.

He too describes the route and all they have seen but he gives much more detail than his driving companion. He doesn't just say he saw animals; he is more specific – they were cows, and they had black and white markings. Then he tells of the oak and the ash and the beech – not just 'trees'. He knew they were of this type because he could actually see and study the leaves as they passed. All in all he gives a very detailed description of their journey.

The two friends made the same journey, and had essentially the same experience. They went along the same road, saw the same things, and arrived at the same destination. The difference was in the detail, and that was because one was driving and the other was the passenger. The driver had to keep his eyes on the road, he had to concentrate on his driving. He knew the scenery but could only take fleeting glances at it. For the passenger it was quite different. He was not 'straitjacketed' like his friend: he could relax and look around at will. If he saw something of interest he could look at it much longer, take in much more, and see more deeply into it.

This was the analogy, and I was the passenger.

There was one other aspect which puzzled me. My understanding of the Zen 'return to the Origin' was that insight is experienced through Profound Emptiness, but for me it was not like that. Indeed, as I have described above, all the insight never even came in Oneness and yet all the stratum of wisdom was there. Again the answer came to me in the form of an analogy while in deep contemplation.

The Analogy of the Diving Pool

Two people are at a diving pool. One stands on the edge of the pool while the other stands on a diving board high above. The one on the board dives off and plummets to a great depth in the water. The other person's turn comes and he gently steps off the edge of the pool and, without even a splash, goes under the water.

To me this displays two different approaches to the practice. Zen, with its focus on the life-force, collects powerful energy. When the time comes to 'return to the Origin', the practitioner plummets deeply into the Dharmakāya. If through a more orthodox practice there tends to be a more dualistic development of insight, the life-force is not gathered up with such force, so when the 'return' comes, there isn't the powerful 'plunge' into the Dharmakāya. If we take the water in the analogy to be the wisdom of awakening, both practitioners, irrespective of the kind of entry, get equally and completely covered by the water, no more and no less.

Second Bhūmi

With the move to the forest complete, I settled into my kuṭī with the hope that meditation and a one-pointed mind would soon be possible again. Thankfully it was soon to return. Insight at this stage was complete and in a very short time the mind cleared itself of attachment and the energetic joy of release.

While still employing the insight practice that had been with me all these months the mind locked strongly on to the investigation of the self – the self that is 'me' inside this mind and body. Although I received help with this investigation from the abbot, in the sense of help in identifying the labelling of the insight that flowed, what was happening was wholly spontaneous and in no way guided or interfered with by me. What I discovered was that this was the investigation of the Path Knowledges that belong to the Arahant Path, and it was assumed that it was leading to the Sakadāgāmi stage. It was a period of intense meditation, and it was in truth the second stage of Bodhisattvahood, a stage that was to last for nearly three months.

The mind was very refined during this period. I remember not being bothered much by any of the kilesas: concentration was easy and purposeful. It seemed very easy for me to move into one Knowledge, to mature insight into it, and to slide effortlessly into the next one.

After some weeks the final stage of the Path Knowledges (*Sankhārā Upekkhā*) was entered into. There I rested, as I had once before, waiting patiently for what I had been led to believe was going to be the Sakadāgāmi Path. But it didn't happen.

One day while sitting in deep samādhi, maturity was reached, but what happened then was not the deeper entry into the Arahant Path. What was entered into was the deepest samādhi that I had yet experienced. While in that absorption, the 'inner voice' that was to help and guide me so much in the months to come spoke for the first time and said, 'There is only the One.' With that came a sudden change within me that cannot be accurately described. Insight at this stage was complete and the Arahant Path that had been so much investigated over these past weeks suddenly became absorbed into something far greater.

The Arahant Path that is solely concerned with insight into 'me' as a person who lives in this body was gone. The wonderful and marvellous vipassanā practice that I'd enjoyed so much for the last eighteen months had gone with it. And what then returned was the all-embracing practice that was my foundation in Buddhism.

This practice has 'me' as an individual very much part of it, but it also embraces 'other' and the external world and treats it all as one, as having exactly the same origin. One part is not separate or different from another; all support and condition each other, all flow at one with each other.

I would look at the beauty of the forest with its shapes, colours, and textures, and wonder at the monkeys that would visit me every day; marvel at the animals and insects that brought the forest to life and entertained me daily in the bright warm sunshine. Seeing all this I knew that 'I and other' in all this wonder were not really separate, frightened little things but were part of the 'One Mind' in its eternal dance of joy.

In Buddhism this is called the Mahāyāna, and after one-and-a-half years I was once again submerged in it. This is the point at which the third stage of Boddhisattva-hood began. It was to last for seven months.

Third Bhūmi

With the heart now going back to the 'all-embracing practice', the two 'ways' were very clear to me. Now in what was being investigated there was no distinction between 'me' and 'other'. All was seen as 'me', all as a product of the deluded mind.

What changed now I can best describe as the 'spirit' of practice. It was no longer concerned with just me. I saw more and more clearly as the days went by that I had a very close relationship with fellow beings and, in just the same way, with trees, flowers, animals, and the wind and clouds. We were all Children of the Buddha. This freed the mind to expand and expand, and become more spacious, tolerant, and warm. I saw that I was an inseparable part of this wonderful, beautiful, and mysterious life, and just wanted to be absorbed into the colours, shapes, odours, and sounds, all dancing in an eternal unending flow. Then I would be caught in the exhilaration that in reality all this was the real *me*!

Meditation Phenomena

Many different experiences were attributable to this period of strong, disciplined, and concentrated meditation.

The Gandharvas continued to entertain with their music. Beautiful aromas would come to my nose – so sweet and delicate. There was much perception of light during meditation: flashing lights, the overspill of collected mental energy, discharging in much the same way that lightning discharges during a thunderstorm. The body would become so light it was as though it wasn't there at all.

I became aware of the spontaneity of physical movement. We all like to think, 'It is me that moves my arms and legs and body,' but we are wrong. It was quite wonderful to see that in truth it isn't me at all that does this. After all, there isn't a 'me', remember? The truth is, it's all just magic!

While in samādhi, there can sometimes be a vigorous shaking of the head. This happens because the life-force, being more liberated, flows freely and more quickly through the chakras and their channels. But because the 'exit' chakra at the back of the head is not opened enough, the force expels itself with this shaking. This shaking never bothers me, I am only aware of it when someone reminds me of it.

Many different phenomena can arise because of this concentrated energy. It becomes refined, pure, and very powerful. Basically, anything can happen when it is in this state, but there is never any need for concern.

Fourth Bhūmi

As the third stage came to an end, the life-force, or heart energy, was collected and concentrated – not just mentally but physically. Mind and body felt like one ball of contained, controlled energy. Soon the fourth stage of Bodhisattvahood would begin, and this would take me into the most dangerous, fearful, and difficult period of my life. But for the help of the 'inner voice', it could easily have ended in disaster.

It all began with a build-up of the life-force in the hara. My experience is that this always means that something is about to 'give'. It is usually a painful experience, as gathering takes place 'at the seat of the emotions', but it is a sign of right practice. It is a time when real change can take place – when it 'breaks'. But equally it is a time of danger because of the power that wants to burst. Experience of practice is essential here, and the ability to contain that power, for if it is let loose it can be very damaging indeed.

The build-up continued, and one day māra arrived, that little devil that is in all of us, that comes to us whenever there is a situation he feels he can exploit, so that he can increase his position just a little bit more. The situation was right for him, with all this power just waiting to explode. So he came, and for the next six weeks he laid into me with hateful vengeance, the like of which I had never experienced before.

He latched on to a small rule which I sometimes broke, but which was really not very important. The mind broke into two halves: one half, totally possessed by māra, had nothing but hatred and contempt for me and my hypocrisy and impure practice; the other half tried to reason, defend, and contain this onslaught.

Māra didn't let up. He tried with all his might and cunning to get me to let loose the tremendous power that consumed my whole being, battling the whole time with the part of me that brought forth insight, the part that says 'Don't react, just accept.' The intensity just never let up.

What came continually to my mind was the image of the little girl in the film *The Exorcist*, who was possessed by the devil, and the torture and torment she went through. It was just like that for me. It really did take all my years of experience to keep myself contained. What was patently obvious was that I was a walking time-bomb. If for just one second I let go, the energy inside me would gush forth and it would be impossible to harness it again. All I could picture was me running through the forest, screaming, with my mind completely shattered.

I could easily have fallen into the delusion that this creature came from outside of me, for it was quite happy to finish my life, but I never once saw it like that. The battle was always seen as a product of my own deluded mind.

I felt cut open. With all these terrible thoughts coming up from the great depths of the subconscious I felt very vulnerable and near to despair.

Since my Dharma practice began, I have always had a wonderful relationship and rapport with the Dharma itself. I would talk to it, pray to it, sometimes even curse it when I didn't get my own way. I always felt protected by it as it guided me so skilfully through each new situation and experience along the Path. I always trusted that each new twist in my life, however unexpected, would work out okay, and so it always proved to be. Not once did it let me down. Now I needed help like never before. I opened myself to the Dharma, bowed, and asked for help, and it came.

It came in the form of the 'inner voice', the link between me and the Buddha. It spoke many times, usually in meditation. There would be a total absorption of awareness, and complete communion would take place. It would speak some words, and after 'returning' I would contemplate those words; its wisdom was so profound that at times I would be dumbstruck. Strangely, I would forget the words very quickly; it seemed they were created just for those moments and that situation, and then melted away. Generally the voice gave me the support and comfort that I needed, and offered words that would simply disarm māra time and time again.

The voice is the voice of the Buddha(Dharma). At times of great need it will speak, but only if those in need have the genuine humility to surrender themselves to that which they know is far greater than themselves. The 'Skilful Means' of the Buddha is to speak in the tongue of the one who has surrendered. The Buddha is not a person, god, or thing, but the Eternal Living Principle that is all that Is. When we truly surrender to him we commune with him and become one with him, and in return he shows love, compassion, and wisdom, because that is what he is, and nothing else.

One day during this time communion was so complete that the voice spoke while I was bowing. It told me to ask for forgiveness, to ask the All-Compassionate One to forgive my sins and weaknesses and to help me in my efforts to overcome them, and then with all humility to ask him to accept me into his being. The voice said I should say it like this: as I bowed the first time, it told me to say 'Please forgive me,' at the second bow, 'Please help me,' and at the third bow, 'Please accept me.'

It is a practice that I have continued to this day.

After many weeks of mental conflict, peace came quite unexpectedly. The mind suddenly became still, and māra was gone. Then a deep seeing arose that all that conflict from the very beginning simply didn't exist. It was a play of the mind. Everything is just okay. In Truth, there is only peace.

Two days passed before I realized that a shift had taken place in the mind, a very profound shift that to this day has not altered. It will not slide back again in this life. It is permanent and won.

Although these experiences are a part of the Bodhisattva Path, in essence the practice is no different for any practitioner of the Way. The difference is only in the clarity of understanding.

I once heard a monk say 'It is impossible to love anyone until you can love yourself.' This struck me very deeply, and I have never forgotten it. Conflict reaches its pinnacle just here at the fourth bhūmi. It is māra's last great effort at this level of ignorance to maintain his hold and power.

With self-hatred and disgust our minds are split right down the middle. One half grinds relentlessly into the other, creating much pain and suffering as the other half defends itself – sometimes with logic and reason, sometimes fighting back with equal venom, and sometimes agreeing and buckling under the onslaught, generating still more self-disgust and worthlessness. Is this not the way our minds so often work? Like two armies on the battlefield, relentlessly attacking and defending. Is this not what takes us so near the edge of despair? What makes it worse is that we have little or no control over this mental onslaught. The battle was at its peak at this stage, but clarity of mind was bright, and the 'weapon' that was to bring the final victory was fashioned.

The 'weapon' used here is the same as is used in practice – the 'weapon' of acceptance. When the mind would strike out, instead of reacting in the usual way I accepted it in a spirit of openness – not moving to the left or right but looking straight ahead as it all came towards me. Not thinking 'like/dislike', 'good/bad', 'right/wrong', 'pure/impure'. Opening up to it, embracing it, becoming intimate with it, without reacting to it, until it burned itself out. This act – this 'act' of no act – is to be practised over and over again. This is the 'Weapon of Dharma' that will win the 'Holy War'. It is the practice that extinguishes the fires of greed, hatred, and delusion. It is the practice that stops the Wheel of life and death from turning. It is the practice that brings suffering to an end.

This is how we love ourselves. Not the 'love' of vanity, but the love of accepting ourselves just the way we are, seeing openly and clearly all our faults and imperfections, without judgement and reactions, and accepting it all. This is the platform for insight. When the ripples of conflict are stilled, the cutting edge of wisdom can slice through the bonds of ignorance.

When the peace that completed stage four came, the 'self-conflict' of the mind died. It is now impossible for me under any circumstances to enter into mental conflict with myself.

With this laid to rest, a great 'steel barrier' is broken, and entry into the Mahāyāna proper is begun.

Bowing

Bowing, like chanting and ceremony in general, is of paramount importance to the practice. We Westerners, with our developed intellect, tend to dismiss this side of Buddhism as not necessary for practice and insight. We prefer to leave it to the Easterners, with their inclination to superstition and mysticism. This is a grave error. Dharma practice is essentially of the heart, not the head. The spirit has to be cultivated there, the spirit of practice that learns to open up to something far greater than 'me', vast and unknowable.

To bow the head is the most profound part of practice, if done correctly. This is the bowing that offers up all of me, with all its many sides, not forgetting the practice, with all its knowledge and understanding. It is essential not to forget this part, as we know that it too will become just another possession of the self. Everything, but everything, has to be given up, and that must include the 'giver' as well. This laying down, for me, is done by repeating silently the above three lines. At that time, all is gathered up with a one-pointed mind and offered to the Buddha.

This nurtures a spirit of intimacy and trust with the Dharma itself, an acceptance and communion with something warm, mysterious, wonderful, compassionate and loving, awesome and great. With this growing familiarity and trust we can learn to let go of ourselves and let the Dharma carry us through our daily life within the eternal flow.

I have tried to offer you my experience in the forest during my time of utter desolation. It is because that spirit had been nurtured over a long period of time that I could let go, and in that letting go allow the Dharma to carry me through the grave danger.

If we cannot nurture this spirit, we will for all eternity stay locked in the prison of life and death, and be subject to everlasting suffering. Only when we have surrendered ourselves completely is the door to wonderful enlightenment unlocked, which will then let the Dharma flow through, to break the root of ignorance.

Fifth Bhūmi

There was a feeling that at the climax of stage four the top of a great mountain had been reached, and that from now on it was going to be downhill. Complacency mustn't set in, but it is an undeniable feeling.

Insight was complete at this stage, and with this slice of ignorance finally laid to rest the mind was for the first time free to begin to investigate other beings. With this came the start of the fifth stage of Bodhisattvahood, and the Bodhisattva's job of 'liberating beings' could begin.

At this stage the Mahāyāna is really entered into. Gone is the concern with the delusion of self. The mind now turns 'outwards' into the world of sentient beings and its relationship with them.

As usual, concentration was very strong and deep, to the extent that one day there was a deep penetration into the Dharmakāya. On arising from meditation, self and other dissolved. 'What arose?' came the question and tears of joy welled up again. Profound Emptiness realized itself. While walking through the forest, 'infinity cries, trees blossom in spring.'

A pattern formed that was to last well into the sixth stage, a pattern that sets up an object of meditation (*kammaṭṭhāna*) and investigates it. That then matures and turns into Understanding, which then falls away to be replaced by the next 'layer'. It is a process that followed a quite uncannily precise timetable. At this stage it consisted of four days of investigation followed by deep insight and cessation, then three days' 'rest', to be followed by a new round.

For me the kammaṭṭhāna was a monk, a friend I was very fond of, although he had one or two characteristics that at times were difficult for me to accept. My negative feelings towards him came to the fore, indeed at times they amounted to really quite strong aversion. So the stage was set: me and my friend, and my aversion.

Note once again the shift in insight. No longer was the Mind concerned with 'me' and how it was constructed in the deluded mind, and all the insight that dismantled that delusion. It was now 'out there' with the link between me and other. Imaginary scenarios (concerning me and my friend) would come to my mind over and over again, and the aversion would be very much the theme of my relationship with him as I tore into him in my mind. It was very reminiscent of stage four, but this time the aversion was towards 'someone else'.

Each episode would run its course, and usually it was very unpleasant. Yet the approach was the same as always, one of accepting the situation and embracing the ever present emotional turmoil. And through it all the Mind watched and investigated unremittingly, with boundless vigour and intensity. This would continue for four days and on that last day, suddenly, from the depths of the subconscious, the song 'All You Need is Love' would well up, and it would sing out over and over again, bringing much joy and happiness.

From inside this joy it could be seen with great clarity that this man, like me, was a product of my own mind. This man did not exist outside of this mind. 'Other people' were nothing but the product of my own mind falling into duality, creating conflict and delusion and desire. With this insight peace would come and the episode would fade away.

The song, like everything else, had nothing to do with me. It never came from the mind but from the great depths, and it added the warmth of the human heart to the process of insight. I saw that to 'get to the bottom' of life, love and compassion have to be cultivated – love being the mysterious hallmark of all that is, and compassion that which cultivates the return to full awareness of love.

This cycle repeated itself time and time again. Round and round it went for something like five months until it finally faded away, consumed in insight that was now complete at this stage – insight that showed yet again that it is a practice of acceptance and embracing, and a willingness to be burned up in the fires of the emotions.

The die was now cast. It became clearer and clearer that everything in this great big beautiful world of trees, rivers, and mountains is only a creation of the mind. But the noteworthy thing was that the insight concentrated very much on sentient beings. Our preoccupation with them more than anything goes to make up our minds. Almost all desires, aversions, and delusions are directed towards other people. They are the most important part of the experiences in life. The mind in its eternal chattering is nearly always caught up, in one way or another, with people. The rest is mostly incidental, and to an extent controllable.

Now, whether having direct or indirect contact with them, it is seen that people under all circumstances are, in reality, literally our own creation. They are a play of the mind (*māyā*) and are non-existent. With this maturing knowledge, it becomes more and more possible to let them die where they are born. Instead of bringing them into the world and getting entangled in them, they can now be sent to peace and liberation, and their Nirvāṇa.

After a few weeks of quiet reflection the Mind went into intensive investigation again. It was largely a matter of going over knowledge attained over the previous months, but for the first time it took a metaphysical turn. The skandhas were brought to the fore and investigated to an intensity not hitherto experienced.

Investigation was mainly into the viññānas. Each consciousness was dissected and thoroughly investigated as to its relationship with the outside world. The mental energy used would leave me quite exhausted, but it was impossible to rest. Every single question that would come to mind had to be answered. Nothing could be left out or sidestepped. Until everything had been answered and thoroughly digested, it was impossible to move on.

I would like to express my eternal gratitude here to Suzuki's *Studies in the Laṅkāvatāra Sūtra*, which I was fortunate enough to find at that time. It helped me to orient myself within these particular investigations. This was in no way an intellectual period, but one of deep insight on many levels – so many that at times it was necessary to sift them all, seeing each insight as a piece in a giant jigsaw puzzle that had to interlock with harmony and perfection. It is also appropriate here to express my gratitude to the wonder of the Buddhist scriptures in general, which have so many virtues, but none greater than to offer themselves to someone who needs help to clarify and 'tick off' insights to affirm its genuineness.

It is at about this time, in the middle bhūmis, that the two great Mahāyāna philosophies of the Yogācāra and the Madhyamaka schools are seen. The Masters who gave us these great teachings didn't invent them out of their wisdom, but with their wisdom and intelligence they articulated and formulated what is seen at this stage. All is seen quite clearly at this time as a part of the natural unfolding of insight.

This intense period was to take me into the middle of 1983. Insight was complete at this stage when it had all been digested and 'put in its place'. This digestion is not an intellectual one but more like the feeling you have after consuming a satisfying meal. All you can say, with your hands on your belly, is 'Ahhh!'

Sixth Bhūmi

Soon the sixth stage of Bodhisattvahood was to begin, with a period of investigation into the Paṭiccasamuppāda that by comparison made the last investigation seem thoroughly pedestrian.

One day, during meditation, there came a deep insight into the reality of the mind. This insight was so deep that it 'pulled the trigger' that started a thorough and comprehensive investigation into the construction of the Wheel of Causation. It was an investigation that was to last without a break for the next year-and-a-half, and spanned the time that I disrobed.

The investigating/observing Mind would set up the Wheel in the mind's eye and slowly begin to rotate it, and then investigate each section as it passed, sometimes dwelling on certain parts, sometimes on whole sections. This investigation was deeply intense and unremitting to the extent that it paid no attention to posture, not even to sleep.

I must mention again that this had nothing to do with me! I had no control whatsoever over the pattern or nature of investigation. It was a natural process, with me again just a willing passenger on the journey into the mysteries of the Buddha.

The focus that the Mind used to investigate the Wheel was the dualistic nature of the mind. It was seen at each section that not only is everything mind-made, but it is dualistic by nature: a series of opposites – not entities on their own standing independently, as our minds would have us believe – but dependent on each other, not just for support but for their very existence. Each is half of a pair, supporting not only its partner, but also half of yet another pair, and so on *ad infinitum.* Each link depends on, and gives rise to, another link. 'Reality' is seriously undermined with this insight. The Mind would continually 'rub out' one side of a pair to see its partner vanish, which would then undermine the next link.

It was not simply a case of destroying one link and watching the rest fall like dominoes. It doesn't work in such simple terms because the Mind, although knowing the truth, still gets continually trapped into believing things to be real and separate dharmas. An eternity of habit-making doesn't give up that easily. So it has to burrow ever deeper, with persistence, over and over again until it gets to the bottom of a particular investigation. Only then can it let go the delusion, and shake itself out of the dream.

This investigation would run in precise cycles: four days of investigation into an aspect of the Wheel climaxing with understanding and letting go; then three days of rest, when the Mind would rejuvenate itself before launching itself into the next cycle. It was like peeling an onion – round and round it would go, layer by layer, ever deeper into the mysteries of saṁsāra, a wondrous process that was little by little dismantling every 'nut, bolt, and washer' that holds together this all-pervading world.

During this time, almost as a sideshow, the Mind, because it was so sharp and bright, kept throwing up insights that weren't directly concerned with the Wheel investigation. It really was quite remarkable. It was as if the Mind were rounding off so much insight by filling in little gaps, to give a complete picture.

When insight had matured at this stage, after all these months, the process of Wheel investigation faded. This was something of a relief by the end, because of the ceaseless mental exertion involved. Because none of this had anything to do with me, I could never take a break just to get a mental rest. The Mind didn't even rest in dreams. Sometimes insight would take over dreams, or would just flow without pictures. If that wasn't good enough, the Mind would wake me up in the middle of the night to carry on investigating!

Because of the nature of this type of investigation, as each sector finished I often felt that 'This is it, all is now finished and the next bhūmi will soon begin,' and attachment would come – only for another cycle to begin, bringing quite painful feelings of dukkha because it wasn't over. Much insight into the nature of attachment was attained here.

I could see the mind automatically clinging to insight and 'progress'. Even months of disappointment, knowing that it was only attachment and that only suffering would come of it, didn't stop the mind from continuing this pattern. I saw that attachment is just an automatic unavoidable impulse. Even insight doesn't prevent it.

Attachments are karmic impulses that act from habits formed long ago, and are beyond the will to prevent. Ordinarily we are pulled around by them for ever. What is wonderful about practising the Dharma is that we can learn to harness this desire of attachment and use it positively, contain this force until it gentles and burns away that which gets attached. And what is it that gets attached? It is this notion of self. It is the sense of self that is the closest ally of attachment; in fact they are quite inseparable, and feed and support each other. If one day the impulse to attach were truly to die, so too would the self. I think it is important not to fall into the trap of thinking that to attach is some kind of sin, and that one should feel shame or guilt about it.

I sometimes feel that some people use this 'fault' as a Christian might use the concept of 'Original Sin', to instil a sense of guilt. Attachment is as natural as the sun rising in the morning, and quite as unavoidable. Be on your guard and ever watchful; learn to identify it and contain it and make use of it, because it is the precious fuel of practice. Without it, there is no practice. The power of attachment gives the practice its life and its edge, so make friends with it. When truly transformed it is the Buddha himself.

Insight at this stage was complete, and there followed eighteen months in which nothing much happened. The mind was very ordinary again and thoughts came that my puṇya was exhausted, and progress along the Path had finished.

It was in June 1986 that a great karmic burden suddenly lifted quite out of the blue, and with it a blinding veil. Feelings of great joy welled up again when the introduction of insight into Profound Emptiness came, which heralded the passing into the seventh stage of Bodhi-sattvahood.

Seventh Bhūmi

I am reluctant to go into much detail about this stage, simply because it is incomplete. What can be said is that it is by far the longest stage. Eleven years so far.

In broad terms, it is the bringing together with insight of the 'outside' and the 'inside'. The earlier stages concerned mainly 'me' as a person living inside the body which is 'me and mine'. Later stages concerned 'other' – the outside world of people and objects. This stage is bringing about the merging of these stages, which shows that inside and outside (subject and object) are a product of the mind and have no reality outside it. This merging is only possible with the introduction of Profound Emptiness, which destroys the notion that all is solid and real. When that notion is removed, 'everything' merges into one, as seen with insight.

All that has been seen through in all the stages has been a process of observation by the Mind; and a deep and wonderful development of wisdom into ignorance and delusion and an opening up into the unimaginable miracle of life. But it has been essentially an observing wisdom. As the seventh stage moves on, that observing Mind, loaded with understanding, now has to move 'back' into itself, forgetting itself and therefore moving into what it can never know. In Zen there is a kōan that goes 'Before thinking of good or bad, what is your true face?' Now the Mind, with awareness, comes back before 'good and bad' arise and becomes the spontaneity of the form, and begins to live completely without knowing itself. All wisdom (Mind) has to die, along with every-thing else that may remain (mind), dissolving into wholeheartedness, living spontaneously in an ordinary way. When this is fully matured, even this has to go, for it then hands itself into the 'Empty Circle'.

Conclusion

This is the story of the wonderful journey that is being taken, and now I feel the time has come to pass it on to encourage and inspire others to make use of it in their own practice, if they so wish. Most who walk this Path conceal it in their teachings, only occasionally referring to it, and then usually in coded ways. I thought about these writings a great deal before deciding to commit them to paper in this totally open way. It was not a hasty decision; after all, it has been unfolding for the last sixteen years!

The Dharma is new to Western people, and already there are many questionable 'practices'. The journey you have read about is true and correct, it is in no way a creation of the deluded mind. I would like to think that those who read this will gain inspiration from it, as well as use it to take up the practice or redouble their efforts.

What has happened has happened to a Westerner, not some mysterious Easterner: just an ordinary working-class chap with average intelligence and an ordinary education, who carries around as much 'baggage' as most

Western people do, had the good karma to find a teacher who knew the Way, and who from day one of coming to the practice has committed himself to do his very best, without any ambitions, in a consistent way, without wavering; with a determination that is not necessarily seen from the outside as some worldly pursuit, not with the sort of bullish determination seen from the outside – which is so much admired in the world – but a quiet inner determination, that for the most part is hidden and not seen.

Do not believe that only ordained people can attain insight, either; it is not true. I was in robes (and only a novice) for only one of my six-and-a-half years of practice before 'returning to the Source'. You can practise perfectly well in lay life. It is not the outer form of appearances that is important, but true practice and commitment. That commitment has to be complete, consistent, and never a compromise. So find a teacher who has walked the Way and surrender to him – there is no other way, if you are truly serious.

And Finally...

I will finish by giving you the secret of awakening.

The *Mahāsatipaṭṭhaṇa Sutta* says: 'When you walk, know you are walking; when you stand, know you are standing; when you sit, know you are sitting; and when you lie down, know you are lying down.' This means at all times being aware and knowing yourself in whatever you are doing. What you are doing is of no consequence; just know it. With that knowing, you are 'staying at home'. Know your physical attitude, know your mental thoughts, and know your emotional responses. In this knowing, there is nothing for you to do but know, while staying at home. Do not judge yourself and label yourself – just know while staying at home and accept yourself without reactions.

This is like during the creation of a sword, whilst the sword is not yet a sword. In order for it to be a true sword the blade has to have a cutting edge, or it is just a useless thing. The cutting edge will be wisdom, and wisdom means developing insight into your entire being: knowing yourself while staying at home, and accepting yourself in all the postures. This wisdom has to be honed. It is honed through the relentless development of insight practice, which has to be learned with a teacher. While you endeavour to practise, only the teacher will be capable of guiding you through the darkness when your karma comes to block the Way.

Is it possible to say that the blade of a sword is separate from the edge? Of course not! And how can you have an edge and no blade? When the two are one, only then do you have a sword.

With that understood there is just one more ingredient that has to be known, and that is the total commitment to the Way. Immerse yourself in the Dharma, dive into it like you would into a pool of cool water on a hot summer's day, but never get out! Make it the priority in your life. Immersing means developing a one-pointed mind, 'staying at home'. This can be matured on many levels. You can simply think about or talk about the Dharma, or read about it (as long as what you read is useful for practice). In quiet moments contemplate the Dharma; in deep meditation burrow right into it. Develop a one-pointed, single-minded mind and do it always in a consistent way. Allow these aspects to develop, and you are practising Dharma wholeheartedly. That is all, there is nothing more. When the sword is truly sharp, it will cut through that 'tap root' of ignorance – you will have no say in the matter.

I I

Interview with David Smith

Interview with David Smith

When I first read David Smith's account of his experiences of insight into reality and of practising the Bodhisattva path, I had a mixture of responses. To the extent that I was qualified to judge, his description of his experiences rang completely true. I was inspired, but also intrigued: could someone who in many ways seemed to be an ordinary Westerner, a London gardener rejoicing in the supremely everyday name of David Smith, really have got so far along the Buddhist path?

Also, David had written his story deliberately keeping the autobiographical detail to a minimum, so that the sequence of his unfolding insight experiences would stand out as clearly as possible. Whilst I appreciated why he had done this, I wanted to know more about his background and life-experience, to set what he had written in context.

So, late in 1998, I arranged to meet David to ask him questions that his text had raised for me, and which I suspected might be of interest to other readers. I drove to his flat in East London and was met by a man in his early fifties, very warm and welcoming, mindful but unassuming and unremarkable, until we started talking about meditation, insight, and the Buddhist path. On these topics he spoke with great engagement and total conviction. What follows is an edited transcript of our discussion.

VESSANTARA: You are in many ways an ordinary Westerner, but with this very deep spiritual experience. Your readers are inevitably going to be interested in who you are, and your background. So perhaps you could start by talking a little about your early life and where you come from?

DAVID: Well, I was born in Oxford in 1946. My father was a car worker. I was brought up as a Roman Catholic, had a standard education, and trained as a locksmith when I left school. Apart from racing motorcycles for a couple of years, nothing much of note or meaning happened in the first twenty-five years of my life. In 1971 I left home and travelled overland with friends to Australia. For the first time in my life I was away from the place of my birth and I started to taste the world, with all its delights. Unlike so many people who travel to 'find themselves' or to make some sense of their lives, I travelled for excitement and adventure. I had a wonderful time in Australia, living in a big house in Sydney with lots of people from different parts of the world. I took up playing the drums and played in a rock and roll band. Truly good times!

VESSANTARA: When people look back at their early life, they can often see, with hindsight, clues to the direction they later took. Do you think there were any signs in your early life of what was to come?

DAVID: One thing I have always remembered is how I used to reflect on myself an awful lot when I was a young lad of about eleven or twelve. I used to spend so much time wondering about this person 'David' – and yet I could never find him. That was always greatly intriguing. There was this person inside who was obviously very solid, who took the world, and what it did to him, seriously – and yet I could never find him. That used to fascinate me, even at that age. And I often used to think to myself as a child, if I really do exist inside my head – as I'm sure I do – why can't 'I' touch the sides of my head? Why can I not feel my way around inside myself, and when I feel mentally tired, why can't I just sit down inside my head and rest? But it went no further than that until I was twenty-five, when I came across Buddhism.

As for religion, I was brought up a Roman Catholic, as I've mentioned. I found this terribly oppressive and I rejected it when I left school at fifteen. After that, I had no great spiritual aspirations, although I did believe in God even though I wasn't a Christian – I thought somebody or something must have made all of this. But I had my own ideas and thoughts: thoughts about whether this life was just a one-off, and how could that square with the terrible inequalities and injustices that exist in the world? I was basically trying to make sense of it all. But it wasn't until I came across Buddhist books, quite by chance, that I discovered that I wasn't the only person who had these thoughts. That discovery was wonderfully uplifting – it meant I wasn't alone. It was a huge relief, not because I had been looking for something, but because it was nice to have those feelings and thoughts confirmed.

VESSANTARA: How did reading those books on Buddhism affect your life?

DAVID: The first book on Buddhism I read was by Alan Watts, and it was called *The Book*. I almost cried when I read it because it was as though I had written it myself. As I've mentioned, it was a great joy to discover that far from being alone with all my ideas and thoughts, someone had in fact beaten me to it by 2,500 years! I hadn't been looking for anything 'more', but this revelation nevertheless changed my life.

I read a few more books and decided enough was enough: I had to take up a Dharma practice. Of all the schools, Zen attracted me the most, so I decided I must find a teacher. I heard there were teachers in England so I decided to return home, find one, and settle into a serious practice.

I returned to England via North, Central, and South America, a journey that took a year. During this time I stocked up on more knowledge of Buddhism, and also the teachings of Krishnamurti, which I found very helpful. I think I felt I had to get to the bottom of it all because of that instant affinity with the philosophy and teachings of Buddhism. For the first time in my life I had something really meaningful to apply myself to, and that was my original impetus for taking on Buddhist practice: because it felt worthwhile – instead of a life spent just flapping around in the world, totally bemused and angry with most of what was going on, to be quite honest.

VESSANTARA: Were you able to sustain that impetus when you finally returned to England?

DAVID: I returned in 1974 and quite quickly found the then librarian of the Buddhist Society, here in London, Dr Irmgard Schloegl. Having recently returned from many years' training in Japan, she had started her own Zen class, which I joined. I was with this group for five-and-a-half years before leaving to take the robes in Sri Lanka. I will always be grateful to my teacher for her training during these years. She taught me to keep my feet on the ground and to seriously commit myself to training. She emphasized daily practice above all else, for it is this that builds solidity and allows an essential inner strength to develop. It is that strength that makes it possible to surrender to, and endure, our own karmic forces that arise during training.

VESSANTARA: How were your first experiences with meditation? Did you take to it easily?

DAVID: I found achieving the physical posture quite hard and suffered quite a lot in that respect. I was counting my breath for one-and-a-half years as a concentration practice and I found that difficult, as I think most people do. But I stuck with it. You meet so many people who take on meditation, and after some weeks, because they don't get what they want, or think they can't do it, they get bored and want to try something else. But that's where the fundamental error in Dharma practice is made. The first rule, and the last, is to stay with it. That rule applies to meditation, to everyday practice, to your teacher, and anything else you can think of. The whole practice is about staying in there, in a consistent measured way, whatever happens, through thick and thin, light and dark, wisdom and ignorance. That can never be emphasized enough.

If you're fortunate enough to have a teacher in whom you have faith, and they tell you to do a particular meditation, then do it and stay with it. Acceptance is fundamental to practice, even though you can throw up a hundred reasons why you should change – you've been doing this breath counting for six months, you never get past three, it's obviously not working. Your mind will always come up with reasons why you should move on, either in very obvious overt ways, or in very subtle ways. It will always be looking for ways to divert you, which is why it is very important to stick with it. And I stuck with it. I had one-and-a-half years of breath counting before I was given a kōan, and with it my first foray into official insight practice – though in truth I would sometimes go fishing around even when I was supposed to be doing my concentration exercise; I've always found it difficult to stop my mind investigating.

I suffered periods of great darkness in this stage of my life, which were endured with the help of this inner strength which was developing, and also with the kind support of my teacher. It was during these times that I had my first real spiritual experience on the Path – which I refer to in the text. It was this experience that was to continually support me in the future and would never allow me to give up the practice. But for the last year and a half that I was with the group things went very smoothly and rather uneventfully.

VESSANTARA: So, what was the spur to leave this group, leave England, and get ordained in the Theravāda tradition in Sri Lanka?

DAVID: In 1980 I took my second holiday in Sri Lanka, a country I had fallen in love with on my first visit two years earlier. On that first visit I just travelled around, but on this occasion I decided to spend some time in a vihara to get some feel for a tradition I knew nothing about. During my stay in a temple in the forest in Kandy I met a young French-speaking monk who lived there. He took me to meet his teacher who was staying at a nearby temple. That was how I met the Venerable Dhammaloka Maha Nayaka Thera, who was to ordain me and become my teacher. The Maha Nayaka was so known and loved in his country that when he died in 1982 he was afforded the rare honour of a state funeral. He was famous both for his radio Dhamma talks and as a teacher of young boys who were later to become leaders of their country. He lived in the city and concerned himself with the laity, but he had a deep wisdom that had been nurtured during many years of solitary practice in his younger days. His warmth particularly inspired me, and he had a lightness and sense of humour – with such an infectious laugh – that I will always remember.

On one of my visits he was lying on his couch, while I massaged his aching legs and chatted to him, when he suddenly leapt to his feet and said in a half joking and half serious way that he was going to ordain me. '*Me?*' I thought. No way, I wasn't interested in such an idea! And yet while rejecting it as a silly notion, there was something in me that took it seriously – something which I knew would eventually, despite protests, get its way.

VESSANTARA: As it obviously did. What happened to tip the balance?

DAVID: For days and weeks after my return to England I sat with this idea. Why should I do this? I was happy in my flat in London, and I was happy with my Zen training. Why should I give up my life, travel halfway around the world, shave my head, and take the robes of a tradition I had not the slightest knowledge of, nor any particular desire to become a part of?

As I have tried to point out in the text, the answer lies in the relationship that I have with the Dharma. The living, ever-present Dharma can be touched only by the intuitive side of our being. It is an intimacy with something which is warm and wise, with a mysterious flow which is everything and yet deeply personal at the same time. This relationship had been developing from the time I first started my practice, if not before. It was an intimacy to which I learned to surrender. Whenever the Dharma presented a new turn in my life, I would muster the courage to go with it – even if sometimes it seemed against sense and against logic – for it never failed to be for the good. The pointing of the way to Sri Lanka was one of those times.

I could think of many reasons why I shouldn't go, and none why I should – none, that is, except that it was the Dharma pointing the way for me yet again. Eventually I put my doubts and fears to one side: I gave up my flat and my work, sold or gave away all my possessions, left my family and friends and my Zen group, and off I went into something about which I couldn't even muster up a fantasy or expectation, taking just a small bag that contained all that I now owned in the world.

VESSANTARA: And what did you find when you arrived in Sri Lanka?

DAVID: Well, I was ordained as a novice in Colombo soon after my arrival, and spent the next several months at my teacher's village temple some distance from the capital. It was a difficult time as I was living in a poor village where there was not enough nourishing food – often not enough food of any sort. I became quite thin and sick, and had almost decided to give up and return to England when I was given some quite miraculous medicine by my teacher during one of my visits to Colombo, and after a short time I regained my health. After that I went to live in the Island Hermitage in the south of the country, a place that I soon became very fond of despite the quite hard conditions. It is at this time that I begin to tell my story.

At first I determined to stay in robes for just a year, and when that time was up I decided to extend it to three years. It was just after my first year that the 'breakthrough' I describe came about. However, I stayed on, as I had promised myself, for the full three years. After that I decided not to extend my stay any further and disrobed on the third anniversary of my ordination.

From the outside, my three years in robes seems a very calculated act. If it was, then it was driven by the Dharma! At no time since I've practised the Buddhist path have the twists and turns I've taken, including changes of tradition, been instigated by me. I feel very strongly that if you are serious about practice, then you should find a tradition and a teacher that you trust, and stick with them through thick and thin. I have seen so many Western people 'pick and mix' their practice – which will never work. I made the change not because I was restless, or because I thought that a change would be good for me, but for the natural reasons I have tried to point out. But the big question for me at the time was, why should it have been necessary for the Dharma to show me the way to Sri Lanka in the first place?

VESSANTARA: And did you come to any conclusions?
DAVID: I have reflected a lot on this. I was happy with my practice in London. I never harboured any desire to become a monk, and I had no particular desire to embrace Theravāda. Yet it was clear that it was the Dharma's wish that I did so, and, as subsequent events proved, the Dharma was right yet again. Within just a few months in Sri Lanka, the Dharma started to flow through me. Time and again I would ask myself 'Why?' As I have stated in my writings the change to insight practice triggered the flow, but clearly there was something else that was a bigger factor. I reflected time and again on this until the reason became clear. It was because at last I was free from the oppression that the Zen I had practised had imposed on my spirit. This was why the Dharma took me to the subcontinent.

The practice of the Dharma is the practice of the Middle Way, and that means a fine balance has to be found between the opposites of rigid and oppressive practice and slack, uncommitted practice. It is truly difficult to strike that balance between the two, but unless it is found real progress along the Path is not possible. For me in my practice the problem had been an oppression of the spirit. The type of practice I had followed was so strictly controlled that the heart was bound and suffocated as though in a straitjacket, and the Dharma innate within my heart could not 'breathe' and flow. It is easy to prevent the Dharma from freeing itself from within the heart, a mere light coating of ignorance is enough, and oppression is an aspect of ignorance. Yet when this ignorance yields and the Dharma is released, it will flow with such strength that nothing can resist it.

I came to this life with my merit ripe for release, and I do believe that when this time has come nothing can stop it. It is immensely powerful karma that with the help of the Dharma (if they can be said to be two) will find its way to fulfilment, come what may. This oppressive blockage was removed when the Dharma in its wisdom took me away to Sri Lanka.

VESSANTARA: Just to complete the story, what happened after you disrobed?

DAVID: I disrobed in 1983 and came back to England, after a short pilgrimage to Bodhgaya and Sarnath. I now make my living as a gardener, which has given me my livelihood and training ground for many years. I live alone in my flat here in East London and continue the practice with the same inner determination as ever. Over the years I have sought some 'good friends' – for I believe that to have like-minded people around for support and encouragement is essential for practice. It is a requisite that is often not appreciated and overlooked. Despite this, over the years since my return I have essentially practised alone – though on my return I did stay for a short while with my former teacher, and I have also spent two periods at Amaravati Theravada Buddhist Monastery, north of London, as the resident gardener.

VESSANTARA: Now let's move on to the text. To start with, could you explain briefly what you set out to do in writing it?

DAVID: I have tried as best I could to express my experiences in the spiritual life. What you read in the text is a record of a living experience, and I am trying to give you all of that experience. When you read scriptural accounts it seems to me they are honed down so that you get some sort of two-dimensional explanation of insight understanding. The paradoxes and struggles of the practitioner are never included, so they present a picture of ease and simplicity, or of magic and mystery. But this 'dehumanizes' the practice and manufactures an image of some sort of special being who is beyond us struggling and suffering souls. In this work my whole thrust has been to put that struggle to understand down on paper and so make it accessible to the ordinary practitioner. I may be lacking judgement in doing that, and I may be contributing to destroying images that inspire people, but I just want to offer a picture that is full and honest.

What you read are the words of a Westerner living at the end of the twentieth century, using language that I hope most people will understand and be able to relate to. Because it's my own living experience that I'm talking about I don't have to revert to traditional imagery, or use other people's language, to express what I want to say.

Nor am I bound by their concepts and ideals and how they think these should be expressed – I have the freedom to be myself.

VESSANTARA: It seemed to me, when I read the text, that what you were doing was to distinguish between the real and the ideal, so that you were creating something more like a nautical chart than, say, a holiday brochure. What you need from a nautical chart is to know that there's a beautiful bay here, but then there are rocks over there. If you leave the rocks out, it doesn't really help anybody who's trying to sail in the same direction as you.

DAVID: This is a very good analogy in that it clarifies the ideal and the real. The ideal is what is usually portrayed in the scriptures – creating the image of a 'tourist brochure'. What my text portrays is the reality of the journey towards that end state. One of my main reasons for writing the text was to bring this high ideal into the realm of ordinary practitioners, so that they can identify with some of my experiences and also glean knowledge that they can incorporate into their own practice. This is the very basis of the work.

I am using 'western-speak' to give you the whole story, warts and all. Inasmuch as the story is conveying a living experience, it has to include the struggles, fears, and confusions, otherwise it would not be genuine. If I only told the good and the pure aspects, it would create an image that would not find a place in our educated, worldly, and indeed cynical, Western minds. This is why

I like to think my account is all firmly fixed on the ground, and therefore accessible.

VESSANTARA: How do you think people should approach your story?

DAVID: First and foremost I hope people enjoy reading my story and find it useful for their practice. I have given it just as it is – I hope there isn't too much confusion with a mixture of the two main traditions, Zen and Theravāda, and of the language and concepts that I use. If I tried to pull the traditions apart I would be corrupting the story and destroying its integrity. What you read is just the way the Dharma showed itself to me, so therefore I have to present it in this way to be authentic. I hope this natural mix will illustrate that, in essence, the Buddha's Way is common to all schools, and that my story will help to pull all the schools just that little bit closer, so that we can all just practise his Dharma.

VESSANTARA: Some people, having read the manuscript, may object that there is a kind of arrogance in your making claims to such spiritual attainment. How would you respond to such a criticism?

DAVID: No spiritual experience can ever be proved to anyone. All one can do is try to express, as well as possible, their experience. It is then up to the listener or reader to decide whether they wish to believe or not. As far as the style is concerned, I cannot help but talk in positive terms because when, at awakening, the Path is seen, all doubts are swept away, as any related Buddhist scripture that discusses awakening would confirm.

I remember very well that the first thing that struck me, when I started to talk about the awakening, was the positive way in which I expressed myself. No longer could my understanding be expressed with doubts or questions, the way people normally talk about the Dharma. This new-found positivity I found rather uncomfortable at first, precisely because it could be interpreted, quite understandably, as arrogance. It is something I am still uncomfortable about to this day. If I talk to someone who is aware of the awakening I am not so inhibited about what I say, but if I try to express myself with someone who isn't, I have trouble because I know that I can give an impression of arrogance. As time goes by, and as more people get to know about my experience, I suppose I will go beyond that inhibition. The important thing is that I am not trying to convince anyone of the genuineness of awakening with this 'style' of communication. I just want to pass on my experience as best I can, and remain true to it, without embellishment or reduction. All I can do is stand on my experience. Believe me, I don't feel any need to prove anything to anyone, or to defend anything either.

VESSANTARA: And when you dismiss some of the traditional accounts as not according with your experience, people may ask how you can do that.

DAVID: I think your question comes from misunderstandings. My comments have been about only one sūtra

– the *Daśabhūmika*. Because I realized I was on the Bodhi-sattva Path, I tried to find literature that would help me sift through countless insights that I hadn't been able to signpost because I didn't have prior knowledge of the stages of the Bodhisattva Path – or anyone to help me. The only works I could find at that time were scant translations of the *Daśabhūmika*. I assume the translations were genuine, but on reading the text I found it hard to draw parallels with my own experience. Stage one was the most recognizable, and was for the most part the same as my experience. The next recognizable one was stage six, because it is characterized by the Wheel of Causation, and stage seven was also recognizable as the re-emergence of śūnyatā. But for the most part it was of little use.

If its expression does not tally with practical spiritual experience what is the text there for? Or, rather, *who* is it there for? The Mahāyāna is essentially an esoteric doctrine, in that it accepts that deep spiritual experience cannot be expressed in words, and therefore points to it through language and imagery – hopefully, I presume, inspiring readers to go beyond the rational and look for the truth in themselves. This is fine if it's understood in those terms, but if not, if people can't make a connection with their own spiritual experience, they can easily dismiss it as nonsense (as I've heard people describe many Mahāyāna scriptures), or, because they can't understand a word, dismiss their own experience and see themselves as a lost cause! We need the sūtras and down-to-earth accounts of experience for Buddhism to work for people as a way out of suffering.

As far as the traditions are concerned I have nothing but gratitude, respect, and deep affection. I myself am a traditionalist, and believe the practices the traditions teach put you firmly on the Buddha's Path and do not need any embellishment from outside, not even for us Westerners, who often insist on adding extra flavours. If you study the insights that I have tried to express, there isn't one that doesn't fit into the Theravāda or Zen traditions or the orthodox Mahāyāna teachings.

VESSANTARA: Coming back to those insights, why do you think you had those experiences? Do you think you're exceptional?

DAVID: No, I don't. But these things can be very complicated from a karmic perspective. All I can really know and talk about is my commitment and my relationship with the practice – which has felt right from day one. I don't really know why, but I've always been totally whole-hearted in my practice, having a desire from the very beginning just to do my very best. To make progress it is vitally important to commit yourself and throw yourself into practice – and this I did.

Going back to when I was a child, I realize I always had the ability to reflect and question, as many people do. However, that reflective faculty can actually be very de-structive if you turn it in on yourself. It can lead you to think that life in general, and you yourself in particular, are no good, useless. But if you can learn to use that most precious of gifts skilfully, it can become very positive. It can eventually take you to the Buddha. To do this effectively, it's important not to make divisions in your life – not to think this is important and that isn't, not to pick and choose – but to develop the ability to know yourself on a moment-by-moment basis, in all situations. Doing this I learned to see everything as fundamentally the same, to reflect and to know, to look inside without judgements.

If you wish to reflect on karma, and about past lives and practices in past lives, you can, but it will all be speculation. It is true to say that attainment is the fruit of a lot of practice over many lives, but do you know how ripe you are when you come to this life? To think 'I am a useless practitioner, so I must have very little spiritual maturity,' is nonsense. To understand the Dharma is to know about peaks and troughs, and that at any moment the blinding ignorance, that ignorance you think you will never work through, could suddenly break open. It is impossible to know.

VESSANTARA: Can you talk in more detail about the insight practices you followed in Sri Lanka that led to this discovery?

DAVID: If you mean meditation practices, I only followed one before the breakthrough. I had no prior experience of that type of practice at all, and to be honest I don't even remember where I read about it, but I suppose I must have read about it somewhere. Of course I had several years' experience of concentration practice behind me which was put to good use. As we all know, I hope, any form of insight practice has to be preceded by strong concentration. If the mind is not still, to the point that the observing mind and what it is observing become one, there is still the space for the self, the ego, to operate (as it will – that much is guaranteed) and to warp and pollute the true insight. This level of concentration is how I would define samādhi, though I think you will get different definitions in various places. Basically, it is a state in which, unless you make an effort to do so, you no longer feel a distinction between yourself and the outside world. If that is achieved it should be safe to proceed with insight practice.

As to the insight practice itself, I used the conventional 'tools' of reflection on impermanence, unsatisfactoriness, and selflessness. After attaining concentration I would let the mind rest on, say, a particular physical feeling that might have been obvious at that time. Then I would apply one of the Three Signs, perhaps impermanence, to that sensation and observe it along with the mental and emotional relationship that would usually surround the experience. In staying with those observations the concentration would naturally get stronger and, in turn, the observation would go deeper and deeper until the observer became one with whatever the physical feeling was. That oneness would soon fill the whole of me, and I would get totally lost within an intimacy that

brought forth, with great clarity, the truth of impermanence. That truth is inherent within that which is being
observed, and I would know that this wasn't 'my feeling'
at all but something that was just passing by. I could then
apply one or both of the other signs – until the perception
that this whole mass was 'me and mine' just began to fall
apart. That may sound traumatic, but in fact it's like
feeling the bright warm sun on your face for the first time
after many years of being locked up in a dark jail. Believe
me, I shed many tears of joy at this time. How we are
imprisoned by the self!

Usually, when practitioners take up this type of meditation, they are taught to apply one sign initially, and then
there is some sort of systematic discipline pursued
throughout the mind and body – but I never had a
teacher. I tried it mainly because I knew it was the
orthodox way of the tradition. I knew I couldn't carry on
with my kōan now that I was in Theravāda robes – most
definitely not! For whatever reason, I was now in this
far-off land, in a different tradition, and I knew that I had
to respect it and follow its ways.

Of course this form of meditation was an experiment,
but as soon as I started to practise in this new way it took
off in such a fashion that I never doubted for a moment
that it was the right thing to do, nor did I feel that I
needed any guidance. I have tried to describe within the
text the unfolding that took place, so I won't elaborate
here, but I will repeat that it was a totally free inter-

pretation of the practice that had its own momentum and needed nothing from me whatsoever.

VESSANTARA: Did the teacher you were practising under have any role in that process?

DAVID: Hardly any, actually. I wasn't practising under him as such. He had instigated my move to Sri Lanka, and he ordained me and looked after me – in fact he sent me to his village temple to get used to the robes and get some feel for the life I was to lead. I first went there as a layman and spent much of my time learning the Pāli that I had to memorize for the ordination ceremony, and getting used to the Sinhalese way of life. The closest I got to my teacher in terms of practice was to listen and learn from his training stories and anecdotes from his own practice. I know now, with hindsight, that he had more than a good idea of how mature my practice was, so he just let me get on with it. Indeed his understanding was such that when the time approached for my 'return to the Origin' he stopped talking Dhamma completely. At times, when I wanted to clarify something, this would infuriate me, but he would just ignore me or change the subject! Nevertheless, he did play a positive role because of his wonderfully open and loving heart, and a sense of humour that guaranteed continual laughter whenever I was in his company.

VESSANTARA: Your experience of insight is one of the most exciting aspects of the text and you talk about its development being a natural process. Can you expand on this?

DAVID: Learning the Middle Way, keeping up a skilful daily practice, and the cultivation of insight, will all highlight the essential naturalness of insight. Staying in the Middle Way of resisting the pull of opposites, together with daily practice, leads to a stillness of the heart. While the heart is still, we can look into it and make wonderful discoveries about the reality of the self, as levels of insight naturally arise from the depth of our heart. (Of course, it will not be supramundane insight because the root of ignorance hasn't yet been broken.) It is not as though you have created those insights, they have been there all the time, but blinding ignorance has covered them up. It is the transformation of ignorance, to the point that it gives up attachment completely and enters Profound Equanimity, that is cultivated. This state of mind harmonizes with, and reflects directly, the natural untouched state that we call Buddha Nature.

Although insight of this nature is indeed natural, it has to be cultivated and then guarded and nurtured relentlessly. If you slacken it will fade and soon be forgotten, or you may go the other way and consider it to be 'yours' and develop conceit; either way you are in trouble. Only practice that is uncompromising and consistent will lay the conditions for you to cultivate this mundane, but genuine, insight, at deeper and deeper levels.

But with regard to the text, you have to realize that just about all the insight I've touched upon there is supramundane insight that comes from the supramundane Mind, and therefore can't directly be related to the mundane insight that most practitioners would normally encounter in their practice. At the first bhūmi the entire stratum of knowledge is revealed, but soon afterwards the karmic propensities that still remain reassert themselves to cloud over that knowledge. The next nine stages are really the process of dispersing those clouds little by little, until there is a return to the full knowledge – only this time with full clarity, which is Buddhahood.

As this process unfolded for me, layer by layer through each stage, I didn't interfere with it, or manipulate it, in any way. This is, in fact, one of the characteristics of the process: it is as though the supramundane Mind just shows itself – so the arising of supramundane insight can be called wholly natural. By contrast the mundane insight experienced by practitioners needs a much more 'hands on' approach in that it needs to be consciously cultivated in order to assist the natural process. It is not that the natural process does not also apply to the ordinary practitioner, but because the practice, though being refined, is still bound and blinded by ignorance, it has to be led, skilfully, by the practitioner. Ultimately, however, there is only one source of knowledge, the Buddha Nature. So, as I have mentioned in the text, the 'rules' of practice are essentially the same for everyone – and we must never lose sight of that fact.

VESSANTARA: Following on from this, you also talked about the need for insight to be fully digested by the whole of you?

DAVID: This description again refers to transcendental knowledge on the Bodhisattva Path, to the time when a particular aspect of knowledge has reached its full maturity. You can only be certain of having reached that point when you feel a sense of completeness, and only when that point is reached will the 'Advancing Host' move on to the next level. It highlights again that insight (and practice) is not of the head. I've used the analogy of eating good food and the satisfaction you feel as a result of that experience to reinforce the point. Enjoying good food is not an intellectual experience, it is the direct experience of tasting the food which gives that complete satisfaction. It is the same with insight. If you are still nagged by doubt, then it's not quite digested. That is not to say it isn't genuine, but it eventually has to settle completely and go beyond the intellect with its continual manipulation, into that 'ahhh' of a good, satisfying, digested experience.

When practitioners gain a level of mundane insight, they will not experience satisfaction, because there are more levels of insight to attain. If their practice remains true, they will return to the topic in the future, to take the insight deeper.

VESSANTARA: I'd like to look at the conditions that practitioners need to set up in order to allow insight to arise or to mature. You've talked about the need for 'containment'; could you say more about this process and what you mean by it?

DAVID: This is probably the most important question that any seeker of the Way can ask, for it is knowing how to 'contain' oneself which is the key to liberation from the Wheel of Life. I think most people who read this will have some notion of how meditation works, so I will try to approach the question through this gate.

Basic meditation is learned by developing the ability to stay focused on one object, such as on counting or watching the breath, or on some sort of mantra or theme. The object of the exercise is to train the mind to stay concentrated within that meditation and to develop a one-pointed mind. As we try to stay with our object, the mind, by its nature, will always want to wander off, and it's our task to always be bringing it back. It will not just wander off into thoughts: if we get carried away by thoughts, we will soon get emotionally caught up as well. The emotions will of course relate to the thoughts, so pleasant thoughts will bring emotions of desire and unpleasant thoughts will bring emotions of aversion and so on. Soon we are likely to become totally lost as to where we are and what we are supposed to be doing – and so we discover the difficulty of staying with our object of concentration.

Now if we transfer that understanding into our daily lives, we can draw direct parallels with everyday situations – for example, sweeping the floor. Am I really at one with that task in the same way as I aim to be with my meditation? Am I really aware that I have this broom in my hand, can I feel it moving across the floor? I think most of us would admit that, most of the time, we aren't in that state of concentration. Thoughts naturally arise and we lose awareness of what we are doing. Those thoughts might turn into thoughts of aversion to the job in hand – 'I want to get away from this menial task,' – and then emotions of aversion will start to arise, followed by emotions of desire when we think, 'I really should be doing something far more important.' Is this not exactly the same as we experience during meditation? It is just that the broom and the sweeping is our meditation object for the moment, not the breath counting. If we can see that, we will begin to see that if we have a complete Dharma practice (not just a meditation practice) then meditation and our daily experiences of life are exactly the same. We may be prepared to make an effort to concentrate in meditation, but are we prepared to apply that same effort of concentration to each and every daily activity that we undertake?

In order to commit ourselves to that continual effort, primarily what we have to do is try our best to contain the emotional responses that we continually experience in our lives. I say primarily, because to control our thoughts borders directly on the impossible. But by containing our emotional outflows we can alter, and even stop, our thoughts. Eventually.

I have illustrated my point using a common physical activity, but emotional containment also applies to our relationships with people, in fact to every moment of the day. That containment is essential if we are to stand any chance of staying with what we are doing. It can be quite a daunting prospect, because we are so used to giving in to these emotions and to being continually pulled around by them. So, like all aspects of practice, this is something that has to be cultivated over a long period of time. Don't develop a negative attitude towards yourself just because you find it difficult. We have all been trapped in these emotional upheavals since time began, and to think that it is possible to transform and humanize them quickly is to be deluded. Just do your best – and learn to be friendly and tolerant towards yourself with all your apparent imperfections.

Neither the Buddha nor the Dharma expects you to get it right all the time, so why should you? But that learning to contain, and so carry on with our daily functions and human activities fully and wholeheartedly, without distraction, is at the heart of change.

VESSANTARA: Containment is presumably not the same as constricting yourself. Yet you talk in the text about finding your Zen practice constricting....

DAVID: I had practised Zen from the outset, so of course I had nothing with which to compare it before I went to Sri Lanka. In that way I was fortunate in that I hadn't tasted several different traditions and then had the burden of having to decide which one was for me. I was totally happy with Zen before I moved to Sri Lanka, and indeed I will always have deep respect and gratitude for the Zen tradition, but everything is relative in this world and the different ways of practising the Dharma are no exception. Because I had no other experience, I naturally assumed that this was the true and correct way to practise, and all the problems that arose within it were down to me and my shortcomings. That may well be true, but after moving to Sri Lanka, and taking on another way, I soon discovered that it wasn't that simple.

On the meditation front, I had a kōan that I carried around for four years. But to the best of my memory the insight that is supposed to arise through the carrying and investigation of the kōan didn't work very well for me. Its great value, though, was that it embraced all my experience of life and investigated both what was inside me and the outside world. The kōan doesn't discriminate, and it therefore nurtures the view that everything has the same value and the same origin. It doesn't concern itself with good and bad, pure and impure, but fosters the belief that everything is beyond duality and is in fact ultimately one – despite what the mind may think.

This practice, although it didn't develop direct insight, did foster a willingness to embrace everything – without picking and choosing – which is the heart and spirit of the Mahāyāna, and which in turn harmonizes with Buddha Nature. The kōan is a wonderful tool to hang on to when the going gets tough. In times of difficulty, when the mind and the emotions are straining to their limits to get you to give in to them, the kōan becomes something to focus on. It encourages awareness, and this awareness allows you to hold out against those forces – but then any meditation subject has that value. As subsequent events proved, there was in fact a strong insight ability within me, but this type of meditation somehow didn't unlock it.

Broadening the picture out to take in the whole of my practice at this time, rather than just the specific meditation technique, I personally found this type of training to be psychologically oppressive – and this is where the answer to your question really lies. These are questions I've pondered very deeply since the breakthrough, and I have asked myself how on earth this was possible. After all those years practising with a teacher, how, all of a sudden, could the whole insight side of things just take off and open up in this dramatic way?

The answer lies in the practice I'd been doing since coming to the Dharma. It was very good at the outset, particularly at knocking away all sorts of silly ideas I had about Buddhism, at putting my feet firmly on the ground, and at teaching me the basics. But with hindsight I can see that much of the practice that I followed was oppressive to me, in that I found I couldn't freely open and investigate things.

There is a paradox here about the Dharma that is interesting to ponder: it is the most powerful force in the world, yet at the same time the most fragile. When the Dharma liberates itself from the fetters of the heart, it has a strength that is unsurpassed by anything the ordinary mind and emotions can muster. Even though these adverse factors can be very powerful and sweep over the Dharma, they have quite a short life and soon weaken, and then the Dharma can shine through again. On the other hand, before the Dharma breaks free of these fetters it takes very little to keep it bound and hidden. So in my case, because the practice I was under was oppressive, the Dharma simply could not break through – and would not have broken through even now if I had stayed with the group and continued with that practice.

VESSANTARA: Where do you think the oppression came from?

DAVID: I was just following my teacher, so in this case, it was the guidance that was at fault. There was never any freedom to roam and explore within the insight process. I was always told just to forget everything, to stop investigating (with a forceful 'get under everything'), and just stick to the kōan. This proved terribly oppressive to my spirit and life-force. Although I agree, as I've explained earlier, that discipline is essential and that getting carried away with what we may imagine to be insight can lead us up a blind alley, it is also necessary sometimes to wander off and explore. If you then come tumbling down, so be it, just pick yourself up and start again – there's no big problem with that. But if that freedom or that space to explore isn't there, then the deep experience of the Dharma simply won't arise, and I would absolutely guarantee that statement.

The innate reflective insight faculty that we all have can be seen as a baby or delicate child. If you have a child sitting on the floor that wants to wander around and investigate, and you don't allow it to, you're going to severely impair that child's development. In allowing it to explore, it may make a mess in the cupboard and pull a few things out, but you let it. But if the child then goes to the cooker and reaches for a pan of boiling water then of course you don't compromise, but scold it in uncompromising terms. Through it all you still love your child and accept it all as part of the learning process. It's the same with the mind. Don't jump on it because it makes mistakes born from habit, don't squeeze and suffocate it all the time, don't continually remind it that it's all 'I', just egotism. All you will do is develop even more negativity and feelings of guilt towards yourself. Give your mind the space to learn from its own mistakes. The secret lies in the balance between applying too much pressure and allowing too much freedom. It's a subtle balance but it is one that Dharma teachers, and students, have to get right if the student is going to mature.

The big problem is that this oppression can be so subtle, how can you identify it? I am afraid I don't have the answer to that. You simply have to make your own judgement, based on your own feelings over time. The problem with doing that is that your judgement may be influenced by the fact you are having an uncomfortable time within the practice precisely because you are with the right practice – and not because it is oppressive! It only became obvious to me that in my case the practice had been constricting after a lot of reflective insight, springing from seeing the Path, when the Dharma had taken me to Sri Lanka and I'd left the Zen practice behind.

I concluded that this oppression had been the main thing holding me up, but I discovered another factor in meditation that was important in inhibiting me. From the beginning of my Zen training I had been taught that the heart and mind were separate. This is a common belief in the West, and you may think that this concept is not very important, but I made a discovery when the insight began to flow: as concentration develops, our mind, which we consider to be located in our head, 'falls back' into the heart, so the two become one. The apparent separation is part of the delusion that I am this separate thing that lives 'up here' in my head, whereas the truth is in fact an emanation direct from the heart.

The Zen doctrine abhors dualistic ideas and practice, and it states over and over again that 'all is One' or 'all returns to the One'. So it is wrong to say that the mind and heart are separate. This strange notion, which is certainly a 'wrong view', can have a bad effect and be very disorienting in meditation when it becomes clear that the two are indeed one, and you have been misled. This too was a big hold-up, but once I had worked through that and I was no longer being oppressed, the doors quite simply burst open.

The Dharma knew these were crucial factors, and this is why in its wisdom it pointed the way to Sri Lanka. These were very big obstacles in my story, which is why I found it necessary to include them. What can be learned from this is how essential it is to find a subtle balance within our minds in order to practise the Middle Way. That balance is possible only when the teaching we take to heart is itself true and finely balanced.

VESSANTARA: In the text you say that, after awakening, the small mind comes back with a lot of force. That might surprise some people. They might have a view that awakening sweeps all that away.

DAVID: Many people have a preconception that when awakening takes place, that person is suddenly a walking Buddha – well, it doesn't work like that. I've tried to describe the experience as best I can and I can't really add much more, except to point out that if everything were swept away at awakening, there wouldn't be a Bodhisattva Path or ten stages to cultivate, would there? Genuine spiritual insight is always paradoxical, this is why faith is a prerequisite for spiritual training, and why this training will always be for the few and not the many. If anyone has a problem with this particular paradox, it only goes to prove what simplistic views we can acquire through reading books.

VESSANTARA: Another paradox that might perhaps surprise readers is that after your experience of awakening, when your mind was active with reviewing insight, it was impossible to concentrate in meditation.

DAVID: Awakening is not a passive experience! When the heart loses its fetters and escapes from jail, so to speak, it rediscovers its natural warmth and joy, which is very powerful. The heart's priority at this point is to review its old prison over and over again, and to bask in the experience of release and knowledge. On top of that it realizes that all the wonders and mysteries of creation are its very self. The heart sees that it is necessary to hold on to the joy as much as possible, or it could so easily get carried away by the sheer power of it all. For me, just to hold on and keep the joy within bounds was quite a feat in itself, but to go one step further and actually still the mind, to stop the flow of insight flowing through it, was really quite impossible. Again this is part of you getting the whole picture, and not just the ideal bits.

VESSANTARA: At one stage in the text you talk about the need for teachers, and later on you talk about not needing one. Can you expand on this, and say what you see as the role of the teacher and sangha in practice?

DAVID: I have tried to explain my position regarding this in the text. When the Transcendental Mind awakens, the Path is seen. This does away with the need for guidance. Although, saying that, it never does any harm to talk things over with someone who understands. Talking does help to hone and polish insight. But before the Path is seen there is a need for a teacher, and as far as a sangha is concerned, no one ever goes beyond the need for one of those.

I guess I do have pretty uncompromising views about having a teacher, but I have pretty uncompromising views about most aspects of training. You have to understand that my perspective is that training is about understanding the reality of the self, and the change that will take place with that genuine understanding – in other words practising the Eightfold Path, completely and harmoniously.

When I started Dharma training, I well remember hearing the analogy of the blind turtle that comes to the surface of the ocean for air just once every hundred years. The odds against coming to a human birth in the infinite sea of saṁsāra are said to be the same as that turtle, when it reaches the surface, passing his head through the middle of a yoke that is floating on the ocean. It is also said that liberation from saṁsāra is only possible in the human realm. Add to that the odds against coming into contact with the Dharma when in a human body and it is clearly vital to make use of this life. If you take all this to be an accurate assessment, then who knows when we will come to human life or the Dharma again in the future – if at all? How can we not then take this rare opportunity and grasp it with both hands?!

I appreciate that not everyone is prepared to be so wholehearted, or indeed capable of such a commitment. I don't have a problem with that because one of the wonders of Buddhism is that there is a place for all kinds of people, with their different levels of understanding, under its umbrella. But if you are practising the Eightfold Path completely, there is little room for compromise.

I do appreciate the difficulty of finding teachers in the West who have direct understanding of the Dharma, but if you really want to approach practice properly then you need to make every effort to find one. Whatever tradition attracts you, pursue a teacher from within it whom you feel comfortable with – and then trust them and surrender to their form of practice. At the same time try not to make the common mistake that so many people make, of putting your new teacher on a pedestal – thinking they are beyond all your own human frailties. Sooner or later they will fall off the pedestal you have created, and you will discover they are not the perfect being you convinced yourself they were. When that happens you will feel cheated and disillusioned and might well give up, which would be a great shame. I learned very early on to focus on the wise aspects of my teachers, to embrace and learn from those bits, and for the most part put the rest to one side. This was also true in my monastic experience. There is much nonsense that goes on within that tradition, yet at the same time there is profound wisdom within it. So I learned early on that perfect people exist only in our imagination.

When you have found a teacher, follow their teachings and develop a relationship that allows you access to them when times get difficult and you need someone to confide in and seek guidance from. At times the act of

surrender is more than difficult, but it is important because surrender is an act of faith – something again that
we Western people usually have little of. Faith is the
foundation of spiritual practice, without it you may as
well give up. Faith in the teacher and in the Buddha's
teaching, faith that may well have been blind in the
beginning, will carry you forward until faith develops
into your own living experience. This then develops into
inner strength that grows ever stronger until it becomes
capable of carrying you through times of doubt and
adversity.

VESSANTARA: And what about the role of sangha in
practice?

DAVID: If having a teacher with knowledge is the first
prerequisite of proper training, then being with a sangha
(or 'good friends', as it can also be known) is the second.
It is, for example, the bedrock that supports and guides
the ordained monk. The sangha helps create the framework within which the monk practises, with all the
checks and balances that are inherent within it. Deeply
wise rules and disciplines developed over centuries support him and, if correctly practised, together with the
cultivation of his own understanding, carry him straight
to the doors of enlightenment; make no mistake about it.
We in the West are not committed monks in that sense,
but that does not diminish the role of sangha in our own
lay practice one bit.

We need a teacher who is our guide, but we also need like-minded people around us to help support and encourage us in our practice. The Buddha said practising the Dharma is like someone swimming along with the flow of a river who decides to turn around and go against the current. This is an accurate analogy that most of us practising whilst living in the world would agree with. It is so easy to feel isolated, practising the disciplines that we undertake, when everything around is trying to pull us in the opposite direction. The relentless forces of seduction that we daily live with want us to lose ourselves in the world of sensory pleasure and help us avoid the dreaded possibility of ever having to confront ourselves, to see ourselves for what we are, or face the fears and futility of so much of what we do. The power of these forces is great and unremitting, but to be with others who have a similar experience to ours, who can understand, support, advise, and encourage us, is immensely helpful.

There is another value that sangha brings that is useful for quite the opposite reason, which is that it is quite easy, when training on your own, to get into the state of mind where you believe that what you are doing is right practice, that you've got it all worked out, and that you really don't need any support or guidance at all. Coming into a sangha can then be quite upsetting, as all your cherished notions about right practice are challenged and taken apart by your friends, which leaves you, very often, feeling rather deflated! This aspect of counterbalance is very valuable.

To be able to get these types of help, and also just to be able to meditate and be around like-minded people, is such a positive experience that, to be frank, I don't think it's possible to be without sangha for any length of time, and still walk the Way.

VESSANTARA: What place would you give to Dharma study in a life of practice?

DAVID: If you mean books, then Dharma study is at its most important when you first come to Buddhism. I remember I read quite a lot at that time, not just Buddhist books but psychology books as well, just so that I could get some sort of grip on this mind of mine and have some idea what made me tick. In the West we have such complicated minds, and a great tendency to dislike ourselves, so to understand a little of how we work can settle us and allow us to take that first big step into the Dharma. Having some sort of understanding, and therefore control, of ourselves can allow us to let go just a little in order to take what can be a frightening step forward. It is very important to understand – and this applies to all stages of practice – that we need to feel balanced and comfortable with ourselves at least most of the time. When we feel disoriented and lost, practice is not possible.

I would suggest reading books that give you a framework of the Dharma, that make sense, and that give you the confidence to settle down in the practice. I have never intentionally read books that I haven't felt were relevant to where I was in my practice at the time. Of course, you will naturally pick up all sorts of other information along the way. Buddhism can be the most fascinating of all religions to study, with subjects like karma and rebirth, all those mysterious realms of saṁsāra, and those insights that the Mahāyāna especially likes to eulogize. But we need to be careful about this. Books should be seen for what they are and be taken up lightly, not grabbed at as desperately important. Just to go off and accumulate knowledge may make for interesting dinner party conversation on Buddhism, but in terms of real practice it is questionable.

I think the rule with study is to try to read material that will make you turn inward and reflect upon yourself, not material that will pull you to the outside world. Keep it all to a minimum! But if you are really serious about study may I suggest the best 'book' to read, the one that will give you the best possible drama and suspense, the one with all the human emotions, all the virtues and vices, all the mystery and wonder that you could ever want, with a climax on the very last page, and a twist that not even the best fiction writers in the world could dream up. That 'book' is the study of your own mind and body. Why it isn't permanently on top of the best-sellers list is just beyond me!

VESSANTARA: At the opposite end of the spectrum, perhaps, what role do you see jhāna [Sanskrit *dhyāna*] playing in the whole process of gaining insight?

DAVID: It is not a subject that I needed to get acquainted with for my own practice, but it was a popular topic of conversation for monks when I lived in Sri Lanka. It seems that to cultivate this meditation correctly requires many hours of dedicated sitting and walking daily, and even a specific lifestyle of almost total inactivity. Monks out there often said that Western people could never perfect the art because we carry too much karma, which will interfere with and impede this subtle practice. Easterners are very different in that, generally speaking, they have a much less complicated upbringing. They have often had a quiet, simple village life with just a basic education, they are ordained young and generally have not been caught up in a heavy karma-producing life. So when they come to sit in meditation there is little heavy thought and emotion to prevent them from attaining these refined states. While I lived in the forest I was fortunate to live with monks who were proficient in the jhānas and they would often tell me not to get too interested in this practice if I was interested in developing insight. It seems that the physical and mental bliss that comes from this strong concentration can also lead to strong attachment to it. These particular monks were not so interested in developing insight; in fact they would freely admit that they had little of it anyway, but they were really much more attracted by the idea of a favourable rebirth – which is said to be the fruit of this form of meditation. Eastern people do generally focus a great deal on rebirth.

The role played by jhāna is one of refining and concentrating the mind, so that when the mind comes out of the jhānas it is easier and quicker to cultivate insight. Doctrinally, after much cultivation of deep insight practice, enlightenment comes after one emerges from the jhānas, when the mind is at its most refined. Fortunately for us Westerners, jhāna ability is not at all necessary for enlightenment. The Dharma arises in what is called 'access concentration', which can be reached through developing good concentration – not necessarily of jhānic strength – together with the gathering wisdom of a complementary insight practice.

VESSANTARA: A seemingly paradoxical aspect to your text is that you speak of the certainty that comes with awakening but also of going to seek confirmation from a senior monk. Can you expand on this and how it works in the Sinhalese tradition?

DAVID: It is strange and not something I can explain easily, but although there was no doubt about the awakening, it seemed wise to get some sort of confirmation from someone whom I regarded as having the relevant authority – primarily so that māra would get cut off. Having had such dreadful experiences with him in the past, I thought that he would sooner or later try to exploit the awakening in whatever way he could, by provoking doubt. Getting confirmation would at least completely shut him off in this area. With hindsight I can see that there was to be no room for māra. But at the time my motivation was primarily precautionary – and also because confirmation is traditional in all schools of Buddhism.

I had heard of a monk who was the abbot of a serious training aranya not too far from Colombo, so I decided to visit him and request a formal interview. On my way there I stopped off to see my teacher, whom I also considered qualified to make a judgement. At the same time I knew he wouldn't investigate the understanding in a formal way, as that simply wasn't his style. And sure enough he didn't. After I paid my respects he simply looked me in the eye, nodded, and smiled; no words were ever spoken on the subject. The fact that he immediately started to talk Dhamma again was confirmation to me on top of the confirmation!

As to my experience in the forest, that was completely different. Venerable Ñanarama was the elderly abbot of an araṇya, deep in the forest, which was large and spread out. He had around him some very serious practitioners, including several very impressive monks who were proficient mainly in the jhānas. It was a joy and an inspiration to be near such monks. Venerable Ñanarama was probably the best-known insight master in a country that is not traditionally noted for such people.

His all-round knowledge of the practice of insight and concentration was matched only by his direct experience – he was a deeply wise man. His health was not good when I went to see him, but although he was still and self-contained he had a warmth and a welcoming smile that made me feel immediately at ease.

He didn't speak any English, so one of his pupils kindly offered to interpret for me, and the whole interview was very formal. I am sorry to disappoint you but I cannot remember any of the many questions he asked. All I can say is that they were all answered to his satisfaction. I do remember one or two comments that I made, though, simply because I think I was talking out of turn! They were about Profound Emptiness and Interpenetration, two aspects of awakening that we hadn't touched upon. I tried to be light-hearted about what I said and he responded with smiles and chuckles. At the end of the interview I thought I'd leave no room for doubt – so I asked him to confirm my attainment of the Path. This he did. As I have mentioned in the text I was later to return and train at the araṇya and I learned much about his methods and insights. The confirmation he gave was for the first stage of the Arahant Path known as Sotāpanna, or 'stream entry', but, as things subsequently became clear, this Path was actually just a part of a much larger one.

VESSANTARA: The larger Path being the Bodhisattva Path. Do you think there are in fact two Paths or just one?
DAVID: This has been a bone of contention within Buddhism almost since the beginning, and to this day it hasn't been satisfactorily resolved. Let me say before I give my perspective that I do not belong to any tradition

just now and do not feel, therefore, a need to defend or criticize any of them; my explanation will come purely from my own understanding. I have no axe to grind; as far as I am concerned it is all just Dharma.

In order to give you my understanding I have first to talk about the nature of reality, since, after all, the fundamental wisdom of the two Paths concerns the seeing of reality, or 'how things really are'. We Buddhists have decided, when reality is fully seen and known, to call that enlightenment or awakening.

An analogy might help me to explain this more clearly. Imagine that two people are asked at different times to search for a salt pot that has been hidden in my kitchen. They may adopt different strategies to find it, but both eventually do so. They then describe what they have found: a round object, of a certain colour, weight, and material. Both descriptions turn out to be the same because what they have discovered is of course the same object. An object is something that exists in time and space, has dimensions, and therefore has limitations: at some point it came into being, and therefore at some point it will go out of being. If the same two searchers then went in search of reality and practised skilfully, they would find that too. But reality not being an object their descriptions, arising from their individual realizations, could never be the same. I will try to explain why.

If reality were an object it would have the same fundamental limitations as the salt pot – which is absurd. So reality is not an object. It doesn't abide in space and time.

It therefore never comes into being, never spins in the world of existence and decay, and doesn't therefore have any limitations. Because reality is not an object, you may ask how it can reveal itself. Well, it reveals itself mysteriously, through the universe of objects, and in its so doing we see that reality and objects are not separate, but identical. The spinning world of coming to be and ceasing to be, which we call saṃsāra, has its roots in objects – or form – and our misinterpretation of these. The concept of reality (*Nirvāṇa*) is one of going beyond that delusion. But because form and reality are identical, so too saṃsāra and Nirvāṇa can never be separate.

Nirvāṇa can never be regarded as a 'something', and can never, therefore, be obtained or grasped. Because reality is not a 'thing', those practitioners who think that they can obtain 'it' are in for a great disappointment! It can never be obtained or grasped in any way – it can only be realized – through a practice of 'un-becoming'. Only when you finally become empty of every desire will reality reveal itself completely, and if you are then blinded by this revelation and go on to try to grasp it, well, you won't succeed with that either!

So the very important fact to understand about the nature of reality is that it isn't a thing (or a non-thing) and because it is not a thing, it isn't an all-or-nothing experience when it reveals itself. Reality can reveal itself on infinite levels, to different degrees of clarity, according to the ability of the practitioner to clear away the 'dust in his eyes'. It can reveal itself at any time, anywhere;

however, the means to and expression of insight into that timeless reality will be affected by cultural factors. Most importantly, as far as the answer to your question is concerned, it will reveal itself in direct relationship to the type of practice that has been pursued and cultivated. Why? Again, because reality is not a thing; if it were, it would be the same for everyone at all times and in all situations, like the salt pot. In fact it arises and mysteriously reveals itself on many different levels, depending on all the conditions I've listed, and when those conditions are ripe. As far as Buddhists are concerned, reality reveals itself fully at what we call awakening because at this point the 'seeing' is so great that it breaks the 'tap root' of blinding ignorance which then slowly or quickly goes into irreversible decline, thus finishing the endless round of rebirth.

Now we can come to the question you asked!

We could, at least for purposes of explanation, divide true awakening neatly into two halves: insight into self and insight into other. Insight into self is the understanding that, despite all our assumptions from the beginning, there isn't after all a person inside this body and mind that can say 'this is me, this is mine.' The form is simply devoid of any inherently existing thing. After this revelation the practitioner sees that the world outside is not what he has assumed it to be, but a product of that wrongly-imagined self, pasting names and labels over everything that it sees. But now that previous assumption of self has been wiped out, and so of course it takes that world with it. Leaving what? Leaving label-less, nameless forms, or what we would call empty dharmas.

The full maturation of that understanding is the end of the first half of awakening. You could say that this consists of the removal of the negative, in the sense that none of it ever really existed. It leaves, quite frankly, a void. Some would say that this is the end of the story, but it isn't. With the removal of the created world that blinds us, we come to the other half of awakening. 'That which isn't deluded any more' makes the most wonderful and indescribable discovery – a discovery that brings Buddhism back from the brink of being a negative, nihilistic religion into the most warm, compassionate, life-enhancing religion and philosophy, unsurpassed in the world – the discovery of the Buddha Nature.

Not all those who see through the delusion of self discover this Buddha Nature. That is perhaps a baffling statement, but there is a reason for this incompleteness, and it all centres on the nature of reality and the nature of practice. As I have explained, reality is not a thing, its nature is to be fluid and spontaneous and never show itself in the same way twice. It will reveal itself in varying degrees depending on all the factors that I talked about earlier. But the most important of all the factors mentioned is the one about the type of practice that is used to transform that blinding ignorance into wisdom.

There are fundamentally two types of practice we Buddhists employ to take us to awakening or enlightenment; and those practices will lead either to incomplete understanding, or to completeness of understanding. One practice is the sole reflection upon the self that abides in this body and says 'This is me, this is mine'. The other reflects not just on that, but also on 'other', on what is outside, with a belief that all is really One.

Engaging in the first practice becomes a skilful exercise in discrimination, with the practitioner desiring to focus exclusively on the five skandhas, which is where the idea of a self abides. The self is of course not 'out there', so he will actively turn away from the world by disengaging from it as much as possible. This type of practitioner will develop the attitude that the world is unnecessary for the development of insight, indeed it is a great hindrance, so · he will turn away from his connection to it, viewing it as negative. Because he dwells upon this idea of life and the world being a hindrance, an attitude of 'good and bad, right and wrong' develops, and he starts experiencing them as a burden. He sees the need to become pure in order to reach enlightenment, so he has to cut off and turn away from what he considers to be impure, both inside, but mainly outside, himself. In short the totality of his 'self' becomes fragmented – but it works. When his practice matures he will indeed see that his form is devoid of self and the created world of names and labels will cease to exist for him. But he will not discover the full reality beyond that insight.

With the second practice there is still the focus on the form where we think the self lives, but we are equally prepared to take on board what is outside and our experience of that. I think the key is 'the spirit of the practice'. It is the willingness of that spirit not to discriminate between these two halves of our experience, not to manipulate them, or get caught in the trap of developing still further the delusion of duality. It is having the willingness to look into both halves – inside and outside – and embrace everything, to say 'yes' to everything as part of the totality of life. This practice has immense dangers that the former neatly sidesteps – the dangers of being caught up and carried away by all the seduction the world continually throws at us. This is very real, but it is the practice of learning to identify and contain these dangers that leads to the knowledge which is at the heart of this practice. It also develops still further restraint and right conduct, which are fundamental to all Buddhist practices of ethics and insight.

When this spirit of openness and non-discrimination has fully matured, the practitioner of this way too will see that the form is devoid of a self, and the world of names and labels will cease. But then, because he has faced and embraced all of creation with a great big 'yes', without judgement and discrimination, he will go beyond that understanding, pass into the Buddha Nature, and discover its wonder and majesty.

But why is this? It is because the first type of practice ignores the totality of life and focuses in a very one-sided way. So 'how things really are' will reveal itself only in the area in which insight has been developed and cultivated, that is the self. In other words, if you plant and cultivate an apple tree, the only fruit you'll get is apples. The second type of practice, which has embraced both inside and outside, will get the full reward because inside and outside is where reality in its completeness is to be found. Reality in its completeness is what we call the Buddha Nature – which does not discriminate between good and bad, pure and impure, because it does not abide in duality. The Buddha Nature is the mystery beyond self and other. It is also where self and other are born and live from and yet, even more mysteriously, it is never touched by either.

Self and other (both creations of the mind) have no ultimate existence, but you can't use those words, self and other, to describe the Buddha Nature. It is wondrously beyond the mind and therefore beyond the notion of time and space that the mind creates. It does not arise and pass away, but is in a permanent state of uninterrupted flux, and because it is permanent, and therefore unchanging, it can be said to be the true Self. It is the only true state of purity because it is not tainted by the state of duality and, because it has profound emptiness as its mark, it can never be obtained or grasped. It is alive in its totality and in a state of permanent bliss which is love. That love is wisdom in its totality – and therefore compassion, because ultimate wisdom is compassion.

To conclude, the first type of practice will set you upon the Arahant Path, and the second type of practice will set you upon the Bodhisattva Path. However, because the

Bodhisattva Path is complete it also contains within it the Arahant Path. So in truth there is really only one Path.

With that question answered there is another point of interest I would like to mention here.

If you wish to discover in detail the self's true identity and the whole metaphysical truth of being, there has to be an orthodox insight practice of looking into the mind and body – a burrowing to dispel the myth that there is any person here. This insight will not magically present itself out of the blue. In Far Eastern Buddhism the practice of embracing life in totality, without discrimination, does of course lead to awakening and the Buddha Nature. However, because the practice does not specifically focus on the metaphysical make-up of the mind and body, but just includes it as part of the totality of practice, that detailed knowledge passes its practitioners by. To take my earlier metaphor further, if you only plant and cultivate an orange tree, the only fruit you'll get is oranges.

To illustrate this, if you study one of the most respected and referred-to works in the Zen tradition, *The Ox and His Herdsman*, you will find the Bodhisattva Path is there within the ten pictures. The earlier pictures can be seen to point to the practice before awakening, and the later ones to the stages after awakening. Yet nowhere will you find any direct reference to the orthodox Mahāyāna's ten stages. This is not because they don't want to use them, or because they would rather cultivate their own style, but because the detailed metaphysical knowledge concerning the idea of a self, which signposts each new stage of the bhūmis in the orthodox Mahāyāna system, is simply not known to Zen. The only stage one can identify that really parallels the bhūmis is the eighth picture, 'Empty Circle', which is close to stage eight in the bhūmis and symbolizes Profound Emptiness, the dissolution of duality, which is effectively the end of training. It is because these Zen practices and insights never refer to any orthodox and accepted conventional insights, that many believe these traditions are not really Buddhist. This is an excusable conclusion, but if you bear in mind that these practitioners are indeed on the Bodhisattva Path and are therefore grounded in the non-existence of a self, how can they be anything other than Buddhist?

VESSANTARA: Could we turn our attention to look at the situation of Westerners practising the Dharma? We've talked about the importance of including all aspects of your life in your practice, but there seem to be many people who try to make divisions between their spiritual life and the rest of their lives. Do you have any thoughts about that?

DAVID: It is one of the fundamental mistakes made by many people who take up Dharma practice. They think real change and the ending of suffering can be achieved just by learning to sit on their cushions and developing skills in meditation. I guess it is not difficult to come to that conclusion from reading some books on Buddhism, as much of their content is dedicated to this subject. It's an easy and uncomplicated subject to write about because it's a specific activity that is removed from our more complicated everyday activities. We see many Buddha rūpas, and photos of Buddha rūpas, where the Buddha is sitting in meditation – and if you ask the average person about Buddhism they will often say it's about people meditating. But for people who want to change themselves on a deep and fundamental level, Dharma practice is about much more than just sitting on the floor.

True practice is practice that takes place throughout the day, and indeed during sleep if possible. I tried to explain in another answer that there is no fundamental difference between the various activities in which we may be involved during the day, because the whole purpose of developing Dharmic skills is to cultivate and retain a one-pointed mind in all activities. If our practice is to be true, we shouldn't see meditation and life in general as two separate things, but move in the direction of cultivating the attitude of 'staying at home', which means maintaining a one-pointed mind at all times. This, coupled with the development of a strong insight practice, makes fundamental change definitely possible.

VESSANTARA: Following on from that, do you see any particular challenges or dangers for Westerners in Dharma practice? Do you have a sense of how the process of the development of insight is going to be different for us, or of different emphases that we need, given our different conditions?

DAVID: I am not so sure about this idea of different emphases. The Dharma is transparent, timeless, and fluid. As it is transparent we don't need to imitate, say, the Indians, just because it originally came from India – the Chinese didn't when the Dharma went to China. It transports effortlessly throughout the world and takes on the clothes of new cultures in any century. Why? Because the Dharma is the Truth, and the Truth is alive and ever present, as well as fluid so it can flow into any situation. It is whole and complete and wants nothing. It is for these reasons I am suspicious when we Westerners find it necessary to incorporate some additional therapy, or psychology, or whatever, into it – just because we seem to think we are some sort of a special case. I remain to be convinced about that, even though it would seem I am in a very small minority with that view!

From my very first day in Zen I was expected to study Jungian psychology, but it was something I never felt comfortable with. It felt as though an 'outsider' was trying to muscle in on perfection, and it never seemed to harmonize with practice. To me it sent the wrong signals. It seemed to suggest that there was something wanting in the Buddha's teaching and this Swiss fellow would fill the void. Well, I didn't, and don't, agree. The Buddha's teaching is whole and complete and equipped to support and guide even Westerners, and if we can't practise correctly we should look elsewhere to find the reasons. As to different conditions, I don't understand. We create the world wholly and completely with our minds, and impregnate it with greed, hatred, and delusion. How is that different to the world an Indian mind created thousands of years ago? Forget the created mental pictures, forget the culture, just cultivate a one-pointed mind.

As to the first part of your question, I would say from my experience and observation that the great challenge we in the West face is probably something that Easterners have seldom had to deal with, and is therefore quite new to Buddhism – and that is to develop the ability to stay with the practice. This ability to stay with things and endure is so difficult for us here in the West, as we are used to constant change in the circumstances of our lives – where we live and what we do, for example – when they no longer suit us. When we get bored or feel like a change, we just go and make it. Many of us have the money and education and mobility that allow us to be always shifting our horizons. We are often in the mode of change, and this attitude is often carried over into our Buddhist practice.

But how different it has been in the history of Buddhism! Practitioners were born into, and remained within, the tradition of their country, and they were brought up to respect and accept, not question, authority. They were not preoccupied with thoughts of improving their lives, but accepted their lot and got on with it. Life was invariably difficult, but from an early age they learned to endure and accept. How different we are! And yet if we are really to change, then learning to stay with the practice and endure our karmic forces is the number one priority.

But that is very difficult for us, when all our lives we have been encouraged to avoid such nasty experiences!

It is not difficult to observe people wandering around, changing teachers and traditions, avoiding practice when they are not getting what they think they should be getting from their efforts, or just avoiding themselves with their restless wanderings. This willingness to stick with things is the most difficult aspect of practice that we face, because it is going against the current that has been carrying us along all our lives. I remember having this test right at the start of all my training, and with hindsight I can see this was possibly the most important time of my practice.

I started gardening in Regent's Park in London in the early seventies, and from about the third day the assistant superintendent made it quite clear that he didn't like me nor want me in the job, and he began to put pressure on me that was designed to make me give up and leave. If I hadn't just started to practise Zen I would most certainly have resigned, but, because I had a teacher who supported and encouraged me, I stuck with it. I suppose I was not so aware at the time how important it was to stay with situations, but I trusted my teacher so I stayed in the job. My boss was a physically big man whom I would confidently say could have put most Zen masters to shame with his ferocity! But try as he might to put me off, I took his wrath and endured all the emotions that would rage within me – deeply unpleasant though it was. This lasted for eighteen months and, like I say, but for my practice I would have run away long before. Then one sunny day in summer his whole attitude quite inexplicably changed. He came to me where I was working and smiled, and for the first time he called me 'David' rather than 'Mr Smith'! And from that day on we got along like old pals.

I never did ask him why he changed so dramatically, probably because I was in fear that he would revert back again! Soon after, an opportunity for promotion came along and he gladly gave me the job. I was in charge of several gardeners, which turned out to be another learning experience. He trusted me now, to the extent that he even let me plan the layout of thousands of plants for the summer bedding. With this I knew I had finally arrived! I stayed on for some time, but finally left to become self-employed. Gardening has been my occupation, livelihood, and training-ground ever since. This was one side of my life at this time, but there was another side that was even worse than those difficult days in Regent's Park.

I doubt that there was any real connection with my experiences in the park, but around the same time I found myself going into quite deep depressions. Depressions really have nothing to do with what is going on at the time, but are more like black clouds that descend and darken your whole life – irrespective of the situation. I can never remember having had one in my life before, but they are really quite awful experiences. I had several over the next two-and-a-half years, and I remember how strange they were because they would last for exactly five months each time. When one started it was exactly like a dark cloud descending, and whatever I was doing it would always be there, constant and steady, hanging over me. Then, again inexplicably, it would lift – to be replaced by a feeling of light and well-being that would also constantly be there, and this too would last for five months. During these dark times I really felt like giving up the practice because I would blame it for bringing on these bad times, but again I stuck with it.

In this too I was fortunate to have a teacher who supported me, and who sometimes hugged me and 'held my hand' when it got so black that I could not orient myself at all. She encouraged me to carry on and constantly told me that all things change and that these dark times would also go into change – so endure I did. I stuck with it and held my ground through all that came to me, until finally what was to prove the last depression lifted – never to return. In fact I haven't had another since, now more than twenty years ago, and I don't expect another ever to grip me again.

Now that I look back on those times I realize something very big shifted within me, and to be honest I don't remember having any more difficult times before leaving for Sri Lanka.

So this was a very important time for me, not a time of wonderful insight but a time of holding firm within the practice, to the extent that a big chunk of my karma turned over and the Path cleared. This was my challenge, my living experience of enduring and staying with things.

Please take note of my experience – nothing is more fundamental or important than the message they give.

VESSANTARA: Can you finish by telling us a bit about your current practice, on and off the meditation cushions, and your future?

DAVID: My practice now is no different from the first day I came to Zen. I have a daily routine, like most people, and I take that as my framework for practice. When the resistances come up, as they always will, I do my best to contain them and just carry on with my activities. A steady predictable routine is so important in practice because it gives you a framework that you know, and within which you can identify things. It then becomes clear when you are avoiding something. I do my best to stay within that framework; it doesn't always work, but then I note it and apply more effort the next time the situation arises. It is a great discipline and one that needs perpetual attention. When you fall, don't make a problem out of it, make friends with yourself and just determine to do better next time. Just remember it's your saṁsāra and your suffering, no one but you will ever be able to change that. I meditate every day and see it in the same way as my daily practice, and I continue to cultivate a one-pointed mind. During this practice, because the mind is in a controlled situation, I can gather myself up, refocus, and re-energize for the day ahead.

As to my future, well, it is something I don't pay too much attention to – simply because, from experience, nothing ever seems to go the way of my logical projections. It is important to be sensible, though; for example, I try to save money for future needs. 'Living in the moment' doesn't mean abdicating your responsibilities towards yourself and others. I admit there is a desire for a further shift in my understanding, and I will continue the practice with the hope that that will happen, but if it doesn't, then that's okay also. Another wish is to stay healthy for as long as possible. If I am really projecting into the future then I guess it must be about a gardening job that I have in a couple of weeks, and how I should best tackle a bad infestation of chickweed....

Glossary

access concentration: The area in deep concentration just before absorption (*jhāna*) takes place. This is also the area where the enlightened Mind breaks through

Advancing Host: A term used in Zen to denote the Transcendental Mind that matures as the Bodhisattva Path is travelled upon

anattā: No-self or not-self

anicca: Impermanence

Arahant Path: The path of enlightenment as defined in the Pāli Canon. It is split into three stages: Sotāpanna, Sakadāgāmi, and Anāgāmi. Each stage denotes a progressive understanding and each is directly related to a number of rebirths that will subsequently take place, culminating in Arahantship and the end of rebirth

araṇya: A dwelling place for monks

awakening: Discovering the true nature of existence

bhūmi: Translates as 'stage' and denotes the cultivation of insight into a particular aspect of ignorance and of unpicking the delusion of a self, with the occasional fruit of glimpsing the true nature of reality that is masked by the idea of self

Bodhi Mandala: Place of awakening

Bodhisattva: Wise being. A being that liberates all that lives, from sentient beings down to blades of grass, through cultivating compassion and wisdom. He sees that all without exception is a product of his deluded mind. He understands that to perfect wisdom he has to embrace all life without discrimination

Buddha: The historical founder of Buddhism; also the eternal living principle that lives in all that is, that is: wisdom, compassion, and love

Buddhahood: The culmination of the Bodhisattva Path

Buddha Knowledge: The completeness of wisdom, from the nonexistence of self to the interpenetration of formations. Seen completely at the first bhūmi, fulfilled completely at the tenth

Buddha Nature: The true state of being that is eternal and timeless. It is alive in its totality and is marked by compassion and wisdom. Ignorance lives out of it, and from this sentient beings are born and the wheel of saṁsāra is turned moment by moment; yet the Buddha Nature is never touched by any of it

Daśabhūmika Sūtra: 'Sūtra of Ten Stages'. Possibly the oldest part of the larger great Mahāyāna scripture, the *Avataṁsaka Sūtra*, of which it forms Book 26. It is given in full in Thomas Cleary's *Flower Ornament Scripture*, a translation of the *Avataṁsaka Sūtra*

Dharma (Pāli *Dhamma*): The Buddha's teaching, also the true state of existence. Dharma with a small 'd' denotes mind-objects or things

Dharmakāya: Body of Reality. One part of the Mahāyāna doctrine of the trikāya or three bodies, the other two being the Body of Bliss and the Body of Form

dukkha: Suffering or unsatisfactoriness or constant vibration at the base of consciousness

Eightfold Path: The practice as taught by the Buddha which can be divided into the three sections of Conduct, Concentration, and Wisdom

Emptiness: The body and mind being devoid of a self and its creation of the world of names and labels

Empty Circle: A Zen term that denotes the dissolution of the person (subject and object) into the Dharmakāya

Enlightenment: Seeing the true state of self

Four Noble Truths: The basis of all Buddhist practice and insight as taught by the Buddha. Seen completely at the first bhūmi

Gandharvas: Beings who spend their time playing music and are said to inhabit a realm of saṃsāra

Great Deaths: A way of describing the collapse of consciousness at various stages on the Bodhisattva Path. There are four, but a fifth is added as an 'option' because some experience a 'death' before awakening

Great Emptiness: see Profound Emptiness

hara: one's spiritual centre

Interpenetration: Because forms are empty of themselves each form contains all other forms, but still retains its own identity and uniqueness

Island Hermitage: The place of most of my training in Sri Lanka

jhāna: Dissolution of the dualistic mind into absorption during meditation. There are said to be four levels

kammaṭṭhāna: 'Place of work'. To cultivate one-pointedness and insight with the use of an object of meditation, both on the meditation cushion and in daily life

karmic sankhārās: Sankhārās are mind objects (thoughts) which are continually produced by our karmic accumulations.

Karma is the force that abides mysteriously within us that has been accumulated by our actions over many lifetimes. It flows incessantly, producing thoughts and emotions that we habitually react to, creating yet more karma, thus binding ourselves to the everlasting cycle of rebirth

kilesas: Our defilements of greed, aversion, and delusion that manifest in the many ways that bind us to the wheel of eternal becoming

kōan: A meditation device derived in Far Eastern Buddhism whereby a question is asked but the correct answer doesn't come from the intellect

kuṭī: A hut that a monk would live in

Madhyamaka: The great 'Middle Way' school of Indian Mahāyāna

Mahāyāna: 'Great Vehicle'. Many schools of Buddhism came under this general title, which is sometimes also known as Northern Buddhism, but, alas, most are now extinct. The term is also used to denote a practice that develops wisdom into all of life rather than a practice that concerns itself with liberation from the self only

māra: The symbol of evil, unwholesome, negative forces in all of us

māyā: Illusion

Middle Way: The avoidance of our mental world of opposites. The nature of the mind is to always seek extremes

mundane: Knowledge of the ordinary mind

Nirvāṇa: Awakening to Reality

Path: A term used to denote the correct practice of the Buddha's teaching

Paṭiccasamuppāda: The twelve links that form the wheel that turns, moment by moment, creating the mind, body, and world that we then attach to, and the consequences of that attachment. This formula can be studied on a metaphysical level seeing how it creates the delusion of duality, or 'expanded' to relate to our everyday experiences, seen completely in its metaphysical form in the sixth bhūmi

Path Knowledges: 'Purification by Knowledge and Vision of the Way'. The string of Knowledges that lead to Stream Entry, then onward with still more refinement, leading eventually to Arahantship

Profound Emptiness: The body and mind being devoid of a self and its creation of the world of names and labels. Also forms being empty of themselves

puṇya: Stored merit from wholesome actions

Rains Retreat: The time when, traditionally, monks stop their wanderings for the duration of the rainy season

return to the Origin, or Source: A Zen expression to denote the awakening to Buddha Nature where all life originates, and not for one moment ever leaves it

rūpa: A form or object

Sakadāgāmi: The second stage of enlightenment on the Arahant Path

saṁsāra: The endless cycle of birth and death within which we are all entrapped

sankhārās: see karmic sankhārās

Sankhārā Upekkhā: Equanimity about Formations. The time when the mind finally and completely gives up attachment to thoughts and feelings, the necessary foundation for enlightenment

sesshin: collecting of the life force

skandhas: The five gross aggregates that make up the human form: physical form, feelings, perception, thought formations, and consciousness

Sotāpanna: The first stage of enlightenment on the Arahant Path

supramundane: Knowledge of the Awakened Mind

Theravāda: 'Wisdom of the Elders' the last remaining school of Southern Buddhism

Three Signs of Being: see Ti-lakkhaṇa

Ti-lakkhaṇa: The three signs or marks of existing things: anicca, dukkha, and anattā

Transcendental: The Awakened Mind that is beyond the ordinary mind

viññāna: Consciousness

vipassanā: Orthodox insight meditation

Way: The same as Path, but also the true state of existence

Wheel of Causation: see Paṭiccasamuppāda

Yogācāra: The great 'Mind Only' school of Indian Mahāyāna

Zen: A Buddhist tradition of the Far East

Index

The Windhorse symbolizes the energy of the enlightened mind carrying the Three Jewels – the Buddha, the Dharma, and the Sangha – to all sentient beings.

Buddhism is one of the fastest-growing spiritual traditions in the Western world. Throughout its 2,500-year history, it has always succeeded in adapting its mode of expression to suit whatever culture it has encountered.

Windhorse Publications aims to continue this tradition as Buddhism comes to the West. Today's Westerners are heirs to the entire Buddhist tradition, free to draw instruction and inspiration from all the many schools and branches. Windhorse publishes works by authors who not only understand the Buddhist tradition but are also familiar with Western culture and the Western mind.

For orders and catalogues contact

WINDHORSE PUBLICATIONS	WINDHORSE BOOKS	WEATHERHILL INC
11 PARK ROAD	P O BOX 574	41 MONROE TURNPIKE
BIRMINGHAM	NEWTOWN	TRUMBULL
B13 8AB	NSW 2042	CT 06611
UK	AUSTRALIA	USA

Windhorse Publications is an arm of the Friends of the Western Buddhist Order, which has more than sixty centres on five continents. Through these centres, members of the Western Buddhist Order offer regular programmes of events for the general public and for more experienced students. These include meditation classes, public talks, study on Buddhist themes and texts, and 'bodywork' classes such as t'ai chi, yoga, and massage. The FWBO also runs several retreat centres and the Karuna Trust, a fund-raising charity that supports social welfare projects in the slums and villages of India.

Many FWBO centres have residential spiritual communities and ethical businesses associated with them. Arts activities are encouraged too, as is the development of strong bonds of friendship between people who share the same ideals. In this way the FWBO is developing a unique approach to Buddhism, not simply as a set of techniques, less still as an exotic cultural interest, but as a creatively directed way of life for people living in the modern world.

If you would like more information about the FWBO visit the website at www.fwbo.org or write to

LONDON BUDDHIST CENTRE	ARYALOKA
51 ROMAN ROAD	HEARTWOOD CIRCLE
LONDON	NEWMARKET
E2 0HU	NH 03857
UK	USA

ALSO FROM WINDHORSE

TEJANANDA

THE BUDDHIST PATH TO AWAKENING

The word Buddha means 'one who is awake'. In this accessible introduction,
Tejananda alerts us to the Buddha's wake-up call, illustrating how the Buddhist
path can help us develop a clearer mind and a more compassionate heart.

Drawing on over twenty years of experience of Buddhist meditation and study,
Tejananda gives us a straightforward and encouraging description of the path of the
Buddha and his followers – the path that leads ultimately to our own 'awakening'.

224 pages, with diagrams
ISBN 1 899579 02 8
£8.99/ $17.95

KAMALASHILA

MEDITATION:

THE BUDDHIST WAY OF TRANQUILLITY AND INSIGHT

A comprehensive guide to the methods and theory of Buddhist meditation, written
in an informal style. It provides a complete introduction to the basic techniques, as
well as detailed advice for more experienced meditators seeking to deepen their
practice.

The author is a long-standing member of the Western Buddhist Order, and has
been teaching meditation since 1976. In 1979 he helped to establish a semi-
monastic community in North Wales, which has now grown into a public retreat
centre. For more than a decade he and his colleagues developed approaches to
meditation that are firmly grounded in Buddhist tradition but readily accessible to
people with a modern Western background. Their experience – as meditators, as
students of the traditional texts, and as teachers – is distilled in this book.

304 pages, with charts and illustrations
ISBN 1 899579 05 2
£13.99/ $27.95